DARK ELVES

BY GAV THORPE

D1438314

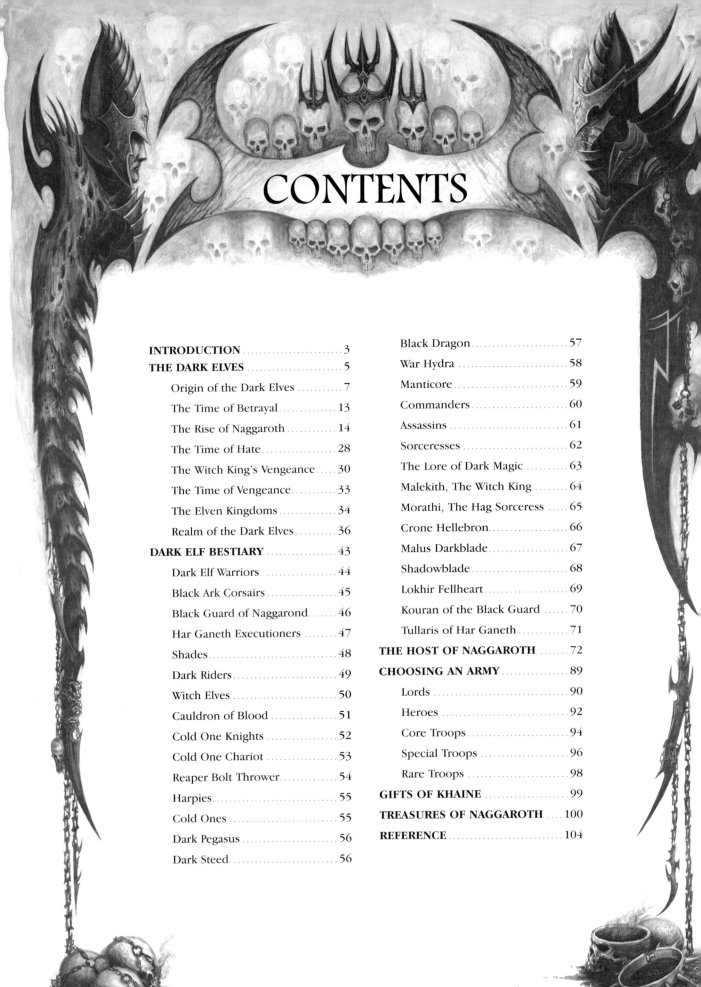

CONTENTS

INTRODUCTION

Welcome to Warhammer Armies: Dark Elves. This is your definitive guide to collecting, painting and playing with an army of cruel and ruthless Dark Elves in the Warhammer tabletop wargame.

The Warhammer Game

The Warhammer rulebook contains the rules you need to fight battles with your Citadel miniatures in the war-torn world of Warhammer. Every army has its own Army Book that works with these rules and allows you to turn your collection of miniatures into an organised force, ready for battle. This particular Army Book details everything you need to know about the Dark Elves, and allows you to field their armies in your games of Warhammer.

Why Collect Dark Elves?

The Dark Elves were cast from their homeland of Ulthuan following a bitter civil war. They are now merciless raiders, dedicating their lives to the infliction of pain and misery on others. The Druchii, as they call themselves, are united in their hatred of all other living things, ruled over by Malekith – the dread Witch King of Naggaroth.

Their army contains many highly-skilled warriors such as Black Ark Corsairs, Witch Elves of Khaine, Cold One Knights and fearsome Black Guard, as well as monstrous creatures including wild Manticores and many-headed War Hydras.

How this Book Works

Every Army Book is split into sections that deal with different aspects of the army. Warhammer Armies: Dark Elves contains the following:

- **The Dark Elves:** This first section introduces the Dark Elves and their part in the Warhammer world. It includes details of the ancient schism of the Elves and the Dark Elves' blood-soaked history. You will also find information on Naggaroth, the bleak realm of the Witch King and his followers.

- **Dark Elves Bestiary:** Every character, troop type and monster in the Dark Elves army is examined in this section. Firstly, you will find a description of the unit, outlining its place in the army. Secondly, you will find complete rules for the unit and details of any unique powers they possess or specialist equipment they carry into battle. Also included are rules for Dark Magic, along with the Dark Elf special characters – Malekith, Morathi, Hellebron, Shadowblade and others.

- **The Host of Naggaroth:** This section contains photographs of the Citadel miniatures available for your Dark Elves army, gloriously painted by Games Workshop's famous 'Eavy Metal team. Banner designs and shield icons are included for the many troop types, as well as suggested colour schemes for your various Druchii regiments.

- **Dark Elves Army List:** The army list takes all of the warriors and creatures presented in the Dark Elves Bestiary and arranges them so that you can choose a force for your games. The army list separates them into Lords, Heroes, Core, Special and Rare units. Each unit type has a points value to help you pit your force against an opponent's in a fair match. This section includes Gifts of Khaine that you can give to your Assassins and Hags, as well as magic items in the Dark Artefacts section.

Find Out More

While Warhammer Armies: Dark Elves contains everything you need to play a game with your army, there are always more tactics to use, different battles to fight and painting ideas to try out. Games Workshop's monthly magazine White Dwarf contains articles about all aspects of the Warhammer game and hobby, and you can find articles dedicated to collecting and gaming with the Dark Elves on our website:

www.games-workshop.com

THE DARK ELVES

The Dark Elves are voracious raiders who ply their bloody trade across the length and breadth of the world. They take whatever they want and will gladly risk their lives for the promise of glory, power and riches.

All Elves are taller than humans and of a slender but strong build. They are long-limbed and graceful, with slim, adept fingers. Their eyes are large and oval, containing a disturbing, otherworldly wisdom that unnerves other creatures. For the Dark Elves, a cold beauty masks the natural attractiveness of their race and a scowl or sneer often mars the pale skin of their elegant faces. They are, for the most part, dark-haired and sinister, and their bleak stares convey nothing but contempt.

Elves live long lives and spend many centuries perfecting their skills. They have deep emotions, feeling joy and despair more keenly than any other people. Many Elves spend their years honing their talents with peaceful pursuits, such as sculpture and poetry. Others turn their hand to weaving intricate magic or fashioning the most exquisite artefacts. By these means, an Elf gives meaning to his centuries-long existence, able to master his happiness and woe. For a Dark Elf the infliction of misery and pain, the delicate art of murder and torture are his only means of expression. He can take joy only from the suffering of others, for a lifetime of cruel indifference and harsh battle has clouded all other pleasures. Dark Elves live to gratify their own desires and to dominate others. They see the artful endeavours of their cousins as soft and indulgent, evidence of a weakness to be expunged if the Elves are to remain a power of the world.

Heirs of Nagarythe

Such beliefs were founded in the prehistory of the world, in the days of the Elven civil war that culminated in the Sundering of Ulthuan. Thousands of years before the rise of men, the Elven isle was shattered by a bloody internecine war between the kingdom of Nagarythe and the realms of the other princes. Nagarythe was powerful; the strength of the first Phoenix King Aenarion flowed in the blood of its people. Their ruler, Prince Malekith, was an unmatched warrior, brilliant general and mighty sorcerer. However, military strength alone was not enough to win the war. Against Malekith and his followers were arrayed Dragon riders, potent Mages and the glittering legions of the Phoenix King, Caledor the First. The civil war lasted for decades, until Malekith unleashed the raw power of magic in a last gasp attempt to snatch victory. When this sorcery backfired and toppled the lands of Nagarythe into the seas, the ancestors of the Dark Elves were cast adrift from their lands and their race.

The exiled Elves found sanctuary in Naggaroth, the Land of Chill. It is a fitting name, for this wilderness is a cold, forbidding land and the homeless Elves fought hard to survive. And survive they did. As the years became decades, and the decades became centuries, the battle for survival gnawed away all compassion. The Dark Elves became as harsh and unrelenting as their new realm, with no thoughts for peace or forgiveness. Hatred, for their kin on Ulthuan at first and later for all beings, has been the frozen fire that burns in the hearts of the Dark Elves, sustaining them through the hardships they have endured.

This is no truer than with Malekith, the Witch King of Naggaroth, undisputed ruler of these pernicious folk since their exile from Ulthuan. Malekith thirsts for power. Sustained by dark sorcery, the Witch King has ever turned his gaze to the glittering isle of the Elves. Where once he demanded justice for himself and his people, now only a cruel thirst for vengeance remains. Malekith would see the world destroyed before he accepts another to sit upon the Phoenix Throne.

Deadly Raiders

Filled with their master's loathing, surrounded by an uncaring wasteland, the Dark Elves look at the lands and riches of others with jealous eyes. They gladly take what they want, uncaring of the woe and mourning left in their wake. Their palaces are decorated with gold and silver hewn from the rocks by the hands of others. The Dark Elves seize harvests, livestock and vital winter stores to fill the banqueting tables of the Lords of Naggaroth, sparing no thought for those they leave to starve. Slaves, thousands chained with terror and iron, labour endlessly in the forges of Naggaroth to mould stolen steel into weapons and armour worthy of the Witch King's mighty armies.

The many raiding fleets of the Dark Elves make this dread existence possible. Mightiest amongst the Dark Elves' vessels are the Black Arks, great citadels that float across the seas upon sorcery and sacrifice. Each Black Ark is the evil heart of a bloodcurdling armada that spreads terror wherever it lands. Great serpents from the deep crash through the waves alongside the reaver ships, while Manticores and Black Dragons circle the skies above.

Upon these vessels, armies of vicious warriors await the time to strike. Bands of cruel Dark Elf Corsairs sharpen their wicked blades in anticipation of the slaughter and slaving to come. Merciless killers armed with deadly spears and repeater crossbows swap gory tales of past glory and boast of the depravities they will unleash upon their victims. In the pitch black holds of these ships, the wails of toiling slaves are punctuated by the screams of those sacrificed upon the bloodied altars of dark gods.

There is little warning of a Dark Elf attack. A magical shadow descends upon the fleet, swathing it with dark clouds. Those on land see nothing but a swift-moving storm. Ships and watchtowers along the coast are overrun before the alarm can be raised. The Dark Elves' prey continue with their everyday lives, oblivious to the danger that closes in on them. Only when menacing black vessels appear off the shore do they realise their doom has arrived.

Fire and death quickly follow, as the Dark Elves take what they want and destroy everything else. All that remains is a blasted ruin and the corpses of those spared the short, woeful life of a slave. For weeks at a time, the Dark Elves prowl their chosen coastline, launching terrifying raids as they see fit. Only when their holds are full of moaning slaves and pillaged riches do the Dark Elves finally relent, returning to distant Naggaroth with their spoils.

ANETHRA HELBANE

When the Sundering tore apart Tiranoc and Nagarythe, those who had remained loyal to Malekith used their sorcery to save their castles, and created the Black Arks. One of these was the fortress of Athil Khairn, which was renamed the Temple of Spite *when it took to the oceans. The ruler of Athil Khairn was Anethra Helbane, one of Morathi's closest allies.*

She had been raised amongst the cults of excess and her husband, Kedhron Helbane, travelled with Malekith in his journeys across the world and fought beside the prince against Phoenix King Caledor I. When Kedhron was slain during the Second Battle of Nagar, Anethra fought off attempts by Kedhron's brother, Hirsunor, to take control of Athil Khairn. Anethra eventually triumphed when she demonstrated her brother-in-law's involvement in a plot to poison Morathi – a plot that Anethra had engineered.

With the aid of her only son, Nurekh, Anethra went on to found a powerful dynasty that has members in positions of power throughout Dark Elf society. Once, Anethra lived in Ghrond and was instrumental in the founding of the Dark Convent. By aiding Morathi, Anethra learnt many pacts and rituals with which to sustain and prolong her wicked life and she is just as ruthless and determined now, nearly five thousand years later. She lives in a great mansion with her son in

Clar Karond, a city built upon her wealth and prestige, from where she controls the destiny of her extended family. From raiding fleets to armies, sorcerous artefacts to the temples of Khaine, the Helbanes are a dominant power that must be appeased or negotiated with by all of the lesser families of Naggaroth.

ORIGIN OF THE DARK ELVES

The Elven race was torn apart thousands of years ago, amidst turmoil and bloodshed. Over that time, the Dark Elves have grown to become the most ruthless warriors in the world.

The earliest days of the Elves go unrecorded, even by their own chronicles. They lived in contentment and peace on the isle of Ulthuan and learned the arts of civilisation and the skills of magic from the enigmatic Old Ones. This paradise was shattered and the Elves doomed to a slow dwindling by the coming of Chaos.

When the great star gate of the Old Ones collapsed, the ravaging Realm of Chaos spilled into the world and a tide of Daemons swept across the globe. Sustained by the roaring magic of the broken gate, the Daemons roamed at will, slaughtering countless mortal creatures and defiling the lands. When they came upon Ulthuan, the Daemons found an island steeped in magical energy and they gathered into a massive horde to devour and destroy the Elves' homeland. The Elves were defenceless against this surprise onslaught, untouched as they were by the depravities of war, their queen a figure of peace and healing.

Yet from the blood and slaughter emerged the greatest Elf hero to have ever walked the world: Aenarion. In him, the mightiest warrior spirit was kindled, and it was Aenarion who would rally the Elves and teach them the ways of war. His heart burned with the dark fires of battle and his prowess with blade, spear and bow remain unmatched to this day. A beacon of hope, Aenarion fought across Ulthuan and in his presence the warlike nature of the Elves was awoken.

Though Aenarion and his growing band of warriors fought hard and long, the Daemon horde was unending in number. Aenarion called to the gods to aid him, offering sacrifices to them for their intervention. Yet the gods remained silent. In desperation, Aenarion went to the sacred fire of Asuryan, lord of all the Elven gods, and offered himself as the ultimate sacrifice. With prayers upon his lips, Aenarion hurled himself into the white-hot flames. Though the mystical fires burnt his body and seared his soul, Aenarion refused to surrender. Through almighty strength of will, he lived through the punishment of the cleansing fires. Purified by his ordeal, a light shone from within Aenarion, a glow of power that filled Elves with courage and caused Daemons to cower in his presence. Invigorated by the purity of Asuryan, Aenarion waged his war with ever greater zeal. Soon he was hailed as the Phoenix King, the reborn son of Asuryan.

As Aenarion's army swelled, the Daemon host recoiled from the renewed anger of the Elves. It was at this time that Aenarion met with the first of the Dragontamers, the powerful mage Caledor. With the aid of his Dragon riders, Caledor too had held back the first invasion of the Daemons from his lands. The two saw the strength that existed in each other and shared a common

purpose. Caledor recognised the sacred blessing bestowed upon Aenarion and swore fealty to the Phoenix King, adding the strength of his armies to the host of Aenarion. For decades the two fought against the Daemons and the Elves learnt their warcraft well. Their natural grace steeled with the discipline of Aenarion, the armies of Ulthuan grew in power year by year. As magic swirled through the world, Caledor set the priests of the smith-god Vaul to bind the mystical energies into weapons with which to fight the Daemons.

Yet for all of the strength of the Phoenix King's hosts, the legions of Chaos Daemons were without number and the magelord Caledor saw that there could be no ultimate victory by war alone. Caledor devised a bold plan to rid the world of Chaos forever. The Dragontamer and his mages would create a magical vortex to siphon away the power of the Daemons and return it to the Realm of Chaos. Aenarion cursed Caledor as a fool, for the magic and weapons the Elves used against the Daemons drew heavily upon the energies of Chaos pouring from the north.

The Doom of Khaine

Aenarion then heard news that was to quench the fire of his heart and turn it into a chill hatred. His wife, the Everqueen Astarielle, was slain and his children were missing. In a cold rage, Aenarion swore that he would destroy every Daemon in existence in vengeance for this heinous act. Though calmer minds counselled otherwise, Aenarion travelled to the Blighted Isle and entered the Shrine of Khaine, the Elves' bloody god of murder. Jutting from within the black altar stood the weapon of the Lord of Murder – Widowmaker, Spear of Vengeance, Sword of Khaine, Godslayer. It was an accursed weapon and the moment Aenarion drew it from the altar he doomed both himself and his line.

Armed with the weapon of the war god, Aenarion slaughtered Daemons by their thousands from the back of the immense Dragon Indraugnir. The hordes of Chaos were hurled from Ulthuan by the might of the Elves. Magical wards and glittering spears protected the growing cities of the Elves from attack and for a while a fragile peace descended. In the ravaged lands of Nagarythe, in the north of Ulthuan, Aenarion set his capital and established his kingdom. Here rose the great fortress of Anlec, a bastion against the Daemons from which the armies of Aenarion could sally forth. Its towers rose higher than any other city in Ulthuan, and five curtain walls surrounded a central keep that could hold ten thousand warriors. It was a city built as a defiant gesture to the legions of Chaos, its black and silver banners proclaiming that these were Aenarion's lands. To him came the most warlike and vengeful Elves, to serve in the army of the Deathbringer. Though his despair at Astarielle's death never abated, Aenarion took a new wife, to bear him a son and heir. She was Morathi, a seeress, who it was claimed Aenarion rescued from the grip of Daemons. Later legends say that Morathi bewitched the Phoenix King, though it will never be known whether this is true or if he simply did not care about her character and history.

In due course, Morathi gave birth to a fine and strong son and Aenarion named him Malekith and took him as his heir. Hunting, duelling and other blood sports became common in the Court of Aenarion and it was here that the most proficient warriors gathered to hone their skills in daily battles against encroaching Daemons. Nagarythe became a land obsessed with war and death and Caledor departed to found his own kingdom in the south, much to the anger of Aenarion. Morathi spoke to Malekith and taught him the secrets of rulership and diplomacy, even as Aenarion taught his son his unmatched skill at arms and gift of command. Malekith soon became one of Aenarion's most deadly warriors, and learnt spellcraft from his mother so that he could wield fireballs and prophecy as easily as a sword and spear.

The Vortex

In time, the Daemons came again, in a weltering tide of death that eclipsed all assaults so far. While Aenarion rode forth once more atop Indraugnir, Caledor resolved to enact his plan for the magical vortex. Though he battled as hard as before, this time Aenarion could not break the daemonic horde. When Caledor and his mages began their complex ritual to disperse the magic of the Daemons, Aenarion had no choice but to protect them. He surrounded the chanting mages with his army as Daemons of all the Chaos Gods assailed them from every side.

Aenarion himself slew four Greater Daemons of Chaos, with the help of faithful Indraugnir. Battered and bloody, Aenarion refused to yield to his wounds and fought on as the incantations of the mages grew in power. With a burst of energy that shook the mountains and cracked the ground, the vortex of Caledor sprang into life. A whirling, screaming tempest of magic engulfed Ulthuan, slaying thousands and tearing down towers and castles. Trapped within the eye of the vortex stood Caledor and his mages, frozen in a battle against the forces they sought to contain. With his final strength, Aenarion flew atop Indraugnir to the Shrine of Khaine. He returned his sword to the black altar and there breathed his last; the first and greatest of the Phoenix Kings was dead, lying atop the corpse of his loyal Dragon.

Ulthuan was in ruins, but the vortex drew away much of the magical energy corrupting the world. The Daemons vanished and Ulthuan was spared. The Elves thanked the gods and praised Aenarion, and set about creating a realm of light and warmth to drive away the evils that had beset them.

The Voyages of Malekith

For many, the natural successor to Aenarion was his son, Malekith. Having been raised in the court of Nagarythe, he was an accomplished warrior, skillful general and powerful spellweaver. He asked that he be allowed to honour his father's memory, but there were voices raised against this course of action. Some of the princes asked for a cooler, steadier head to guide the Elves in the rebuilding of their civilisation. They whispered about the darkness that had beset the realm of Nagarythe, and of the manner of the son that had been raised in the Court of Aenarion. In the end, these doubters prevailed and, with good grace, Malekith accepted the princes' choice of Bel Shanaar as the next Phoenix King. Though his mother, Morathi, ranted and railed against the iniquity heaped upon Malekith, the son of Aenarion was the first to bow his knee to Bel Shanaar and swear fealty.

With the daemonic invasion defeated, the Elves looked to explore the world that had been left changed by Chaos. Malekith quit Ulthuan, claiming that Bel Shanaar would be able to rule the isle more soundly without the heir of Aenarion close at hand. The prince of Nagarythe travelled the world, where small colonies were growing upon the shores of the forest-swathed lands across the ocean. Here the Elves met the Dwarfs and soon the two races were fighting side-by-side, their armies waging war against the fierce Orcs of the mountains and the hideous Chaos beasts of the deep woods. In battle against brutal greenskins and warped monsters, Malekith perfected his fighting skills and rose to become a great leader. So great was his reputation that Bel Shanaar appointed Malekith to be his ambassador to the High King of the Dwarfs, Snorri Whitebeard.

As well as campaigning across the lands that would eventually become the Empire, Bretonnia and the Badlands, Malekith travelled even further abroad. He quested amongst the Worlds Edge Mountains and made war against the primal tribes of men in the blasted Chaos Wastes. It was here, in the frozen north, that Malekith came across a dead city, built by no human, Dwarfish or Elven hand.

He wandered through its ice-trapped streets, between colossal buildings that hurt the eyes to look upon. The shifting ice had ruptured an ancient vault, and within it Malekith found an artefact older even than the Elves. It was a metal crown imbued with powers of sorcery, now known in myth as the Circlet of Iron. Malekith took the Circlet of Iron and resolved to unravel its secrets. It awoke in him a dark curiosity, and from that day forth Malekith turned his will to studying the forbidden depths of magic – the power of Chaos itself.

While Malekith explored the wider world, new travails beset Ulthuan in his absence. With the threat of the Daemons gone, many of the lessons of hard war were forgotten. Many Elves became indolent and selfish, indulging their heightened senses with ceremonies dedicated to exotic, forbidden gods. From the ancient temples of Nagarythe they had risen; cults of luxury, pleasure and excess that grew within the cities and spread across the kingdoms. These cults practiced obscene rituals of debasement and sacrifice, and more and more followers were drawn to dark shrines dedicated to gods that should not be worshipped. Many of these Elves sought to escape the bitter grief that the Chaos incursion had left within their lives. In temples filled with beating drums, haunting pipes and narcotic vapours, they danced and feasted and sang blasphemous praises.

Bel Shanaar seemed powerless to quell the growing unrest in his realm. The pleasure cults were gaining more sway with every passing season. The worst affected realm was Nagarythe, but Bel Shanaar was hesitant to act against the lands of Aenarion's people. Princes caught in the grip of the cults began to mutter that Bel Shanaar was weak, and an usurper of the Phoenix Throne.

Malekith Returns

When Malekith arrived in Ulthuan, he was heralded as a saviour. He vowed to hunt down the cults and exterminate them, claiming that no kingdom would be beyond his wrath, not even Nagarythe. When Malekith discovered that his mother was one of the chief architects of the cults, he renounced her and ordered that she be imprisoned upon her capture, along with thousands of her misguided disciples. Nobody was above Malekith's scrutiny, from the lowest farmer to the most vaunted prince. Those cultists who surrendered were sent to the castles of Nagarythe to be released from their delusions. Yet it seemed nothing short of outright war would quell the rise of the decadent cults.

Malekith asked the Phoenix King to convene the council of princes. He wished to request control of Ulthuan's

armies so that he might cast out the cults of pleasure. Yet even as the princes gathered at the Shrine of Asuryan, a greater part of Malekith's plan was set in motion. Unbeknownst to the other kingdoms, Nagarythe's armies marched, bolstered by depraved cultists and practitioners of Dark Magic. Oblivious to the peril that descended upon their lands, the princes gathered to hear Malekith. His first pronouncement was to declare Bel Shanaar a member of the cults. Malekith said that Bel Shanaar had taken the coward's route rather than be brought forth before the princes, and had poisoned himself before he could be rightfully tried. With Ulthuan on the verge of civil war again, Malekith would assume his rightful position as Phoenix King and avert the coming disaster.

Many of the princes were not swayed by Malekith's speech and denounced him as a murderer and a traitor. At that moment, agents from Nagarythe broke into the shrine and fighting broke out between those loyal to Malekith and those that opposed him. As blood was spilt upon the marble floor, Malekith strode into the sacred flames to accept Asuryan's blessing. Malekith's screams echoed around the chamber, silencing the fighting. The flames engulfed the prince of Nagarythe, stripping away hair, skin and flesh. With a final shriek of agony, Malekith hurled himself back from the burning judgement of Asuryan and his charred body lay smoking upon the ground. Malekith's disciples took up his body and fought their way clear, leaving most of Ulthuan's princes slain in the temple.

Civil War

As Malekith's followers fled north with his remains, war erupted. For the most part leaderless, the other kingdoms knew nothing of the danger until the hosts of Nagarythe besieged their castles. In Tiranoc and Ellyrion, agents of the pleasure cults had infiltrated and influenced the families of the ruling princes. Naggarothi forces occupied these kingdoms. They held families hostage and allowed the rulers to remain in power only to enact the will of Malekith. The armies of Nagarythe were impressive, the strongest military force in the world. Their commanders were veterans of the war against the Daemons and many had been trained by the hand of Aenarion.

The warrior creed of Aenarion had left an indelible mark upon Nagarythe and its citizenry. Iron discipline, backed by fear of their leaders, drove the legions of Nagarythe. To fail was to invite ruin so the warriors of Nagarythe fought with unmatched zeal – better to fall fighting than to lose and face the wrath of Morathi's cultists. There were also those who embraced the opportunity to seize lands from their peers. These renegades raised their armies and marched forth with glee. As anarchy reigned, the Naggarothi moved swiftly, seizing many of the vital passes across the Annulii Mountains, separating the Inner Kingdoms of Ulthuan from the Outer Kingdoms. With them came many Chaotic beasts that lived within Ulthuan's magic-riven mountains. Divided, the Elven realms were on the verge of being conquered within weeks.

The handful of princes that had survived did not stand idle. There was not one amongst them strong enough to succeed Bel Shanaar, for each had worries in his own realm. In the minds of the princes there was only one Elf who could combat the Naggarothi – Imrik of Caledor. Grandson to Caledor Dragontamer, Imrik had none of his forefather's magical skills, but was a deadly warrior and brilliant general. As prince of Caledor and leader of the Dragon riders, Imrik controlled the second most powerful kingdom in Ulthuan, eclipsed only by the might of the invading Nagarythe armies.

At the time, Imrik was hunting in the mountains of Chrace and was utterly unaware of the war that had engulfed the isle. The princes dispatched heralds to locate Imrik and inform him of their decision. Meanwhile, Morathi used her sorcerous powers to divine the intent of the princes and sent a cadre of assassins to slay the future Phoenix King. The gods, or fate, would decide who reached Imrik first.

It was Morathi's assassins that found Imrik and they closed in on their prey with evil intent. Swathed in magical shadows, they prepared their ambush. Yet they had not accounted for the loyalty and fighting skill of the hunters of Chrace. When the Naggarothi assassins struck, Imrik was alone and vulnerable. However, a band of Chracians who had accompanied him on his hunt heard the fighting and intervened. The Chracians slew the assassins but at great loss, and Imrik was

saved. Even as Imrik thanked these warriors, he received word from one of the princes' messengers of the terror being unleashed by the armies of Nagarythe.

While Imrik ascended to the Phoenix Throne and rallied the armies of the other Elven kingdoms, the rulers of Nagarythe acted to forestall their foes. They sent word to sympathisers and agents in Saphery, a realm renowned for its mages. Some of these mages had been tempted by the power of dark sorcery and subverted to the cause of Nagarythe. Though they numbered fewer than those wizards who were loyal to the Phoenix Throne, their spells were enhanced by a new, darker sorcery that was more powerful than the 'safe' magic employed by the mages. Titanic magical duels tore the lands of Saphery apart as sorcerer fought mage. Yet for all the power of Chaos unleashed by the sorcerers, they could not prevail and were forced to flee Saphery and seek refuge in Nagarythe and the kingdoms its armies now occupied.

There was betrayal all across Ulthuan. Even in Caledor, thought by many to be secure against the wiles of the Naggarothi, a priest of Vaul named Hotek secretly forged weapons for the legions of Nagarythe using the magical Hammer of Vaul, which Caledor had used to make weapons for Aenarion.

When he was discovered, Hotek fled and sought sanctuary within Nagarythe. Aided by renegade sorcerers, Hotek used the Hammer of Vaul to construct a suit of armour for the crippled Malekith; although his body had been all but broken, the prince of Nagarythe had clung to life. Bitterness and anger had fuelled Malekith's will, sustaining him through the long years of agony that he had endured. The burning would never stop, and so Hotek fused his newly forged armour directly to Malekith's body. Clad in a rune-etched skin of black steel, Malekith could once again lead his armies. Swearing oaths of revenge and bargaining his soul to forbidden gods, Malekith grew in sorcerous power. He was no longer the prince of Nagarythe; he would forever more be known as the Witch King.

Malekith rode to battle astride a Black Dragon, raised in secret in Nagarythe away from the prying eyes of the Caledorian Dragontamers. Sulekh was her name and she was a fearsome beast, much scarred by fighting, the sole survivor of a brood of eight. Her temperament was evil and unpredictable, and only the Witch King could approach her. With promises of blood and slaughter, and threats of pain and humiliation, Malekith had broken Sulekh to his will and fed her upon magical warpstone so that she was truly monstrous. The two of them were terrifying to behold, and where the Witch King led the armies of Nagarythe victory swiftly followed. But for all the guile and ferocity of the hosts of Nagarythe, the kingdoms of Ulthuan would not be conquered. Led by the new Phoenix King, who had taken the name Caledor to honour his grandsire, the armies opposed to Malekith fought a cunning campaign of ambush and counter-attack. Where the armies of the Witch King advanced, the warriors of Caledor fell back, only to outflank the soldiers of Nagarythe and strike back from unexpected quarters.

Sapped by this constant hit-and-run warfare, the Naggarothi advanced, faltered, regrouped and attacked again. For a quarter of a century, no single ruler reigned over Ulthuan, as each side failed to achieve the crushing victory it needed to secure power. Caledor and Malekith finally met at the field of Maledor. For years they had contested their strength against each other with the might of their armies, and at Maledor they would pit their skills face-to-face. Atop cruel Sulekh the Witch King commanded his army, launching them in an all-out attack against the serried ranks of spearmen and archers mustered by Caledor. Malekith's wizards unleashed bolts of black energy and called down terrible storms to ravage the lines of the Phoenix King's army. In Caledor's host, Sapherian mages dispersed the dark magic of Malekith's sorcerers and hurled fireballs and blazing walls of blue flame at the charging Naggarothi.

Seeing his attack lose momentum, Malekith intervened. Swooping down from the dark skies, Sulekh and Malekith crashed into the Elven host. Purple lightning leapt from Malekith's fingertips and cut down scores of Elves while Sulekh belched forth clouds of noxious gas. Arrows and spears pattered harmlessly from the Witch King's armoured body and the scales of his Dragon. Three Elven princes – Tithrain, Carvalon and Finudel – fell beneath the wicked blade of Malekith and the claws of Sulekh.

Even as the tide turned against his army, Caledor led the counter-attack. Surrounded by the hunters of Chrace and flanked by silent Phoenix Guard of Asuryan, the king of Ulthuan confronted Malekith. The snapping jaws of Sulekh smashed Caledor's sword from his hand and cast the Phoenix King to the ground amongst the bodies of his loyal warriors. As Malekith's spells hurled back the White Lions, Sulekh loomed over Caledor, acidic venom dripping from her jaws. With a defiant shout, Caledor snatched up Mirialith – the Spear of Midnight Fire – from the dead hand of Finudel, and cast it into Sulekh's open maw. The magical weapon pierced the brain of the Black Dragon. In her death throes Sulekh cast Malekith from her back, pitching him into the ranks of the Phoenix Guard. Surrounded by enemies, Malekith had no choice but to cut his way clear and flee, leaving dozens of slain Elves in his wake. After the battle of Maledor, with the jeers of the victorious High Elves still burning in his memory, Malekith's patience utterly snapped. His army was all but shattered by the unending fighting, and with the resistance of his foes showing no sign of breaking, the Witch King made one last, desperate bid for victory.

In Nagarythe, Morathi and Malekith had long studied the blacker arts of magic. A great number of warlocks and witches followed them, drawing directly on the power of Chaos. It was to these dark wizards that Malekith turned. He gathered a huge number of prisoners in preparation for a massive sacrifice and announced his final plan. He and his sorcerers would unbind the magic of the Ulthuan vortex created by Caledor Dragontamer, unleashing the full fury of the Realms of Chaos upon the island.

The Witch King would summon the Daemon hordes to fight at his side and sweep away all opposition. Knowing that their fate was tied to that of the Witch King, the sorcerers agreed to this insane gambit. Malekith and his followers were willing to risk everything for victory – even the future of the whole world. To their minds, failure was incomprehensible; to live in exile and obscurity was unthinkable for the Witch King. He would rather the world ended than see it ruled by any other. Only one of his disciples, Urathion of Ullar, saw the madness of Malekith's ploy and escaped Nagarythe to bring word to Caledor.

The Sundering

Forewarned of Malekith's intent, the mages of the Phoenix King roused their magic to thwart the spell of unbinding. As the sorcerers of Malekith stood upon the summits of their black towers and struggled for control of the vortex, great forces shook the lands. The mountains trembled and the seas bucked and heaved as dark and light waged a mystical battle for control of the swirling power at the heart of Ulthuan.

As night came, the stars obscured by flickering witchlights and coronas of magical energy, the Witch King and his coven exerted the last of their strength. Fuelled by daemonic pacts, their magic was the stronger and the shields of the Phoenix King's mages began to crumble. The vortex itself howled and screeched, and than began to flicker. It was then, at the very moment that the vortex failed, that a new power entered the contest. Freed from their long stasis, Caledor Dragontamer and his mages trapped in the vortex returned to the realm of the living. Instantly realising the peril about to engulf Ulthuan, they added their own incantations to that of the Phoenix King's wizards, and with a colossal release of magical energy they dragged the vortex into place once more.

The backlash of magic tore Ulthuan asunder. A tidal wave a thousand feet high crashed upon the northern coasts, engulfing Nagarythe and Tiranoc. Cities were washed away and tens of thousands of Elves perished. The earth heaved and cracked, and so great was the magical explosion that it was noted in the halls of the Dwarfs, thousands of miles to the east. As the deluge swept down upon the realm of Malekith, his followers used the last of their sorcerous power to hold back the storm. Energised with Chaos magic, their dark citadels broke free from their rocky foundations and rose upon the frothing waves.

Malekith's plan had failed and his energy was spent. His kingdom lay beneath the waves and his army was all but destroyed. Upon the floating castles of Nagarythe – the Black Arks as they would be called in later years – the Witch King and his minions fled the wrath of the cataclysm they had unwittingly unleashed. North and west they travelled, across the churning seas to the desolate wilderness of Naggaroth – the Land of Chill.

THE TIME OF BETRAYAL

All dates use the Imperial Calendar for ease of reference. The Dark Elves themselves reckon the passing of years from the founding of Naggarond (IC -2722). So, to calculate dates using the Dark Elf system, simply add 2723 years to the Imperial date. For example, IC -340 becomes 2383, IC 1534 becomes 4257, and so on.

-4461 Aenarion, the first of the Phoenix Kings, rescues the seeress Morathi from an army of Chaos Daemons. They make their court in the fortress of Anlec.

-4458 Morathi bears Aenarion a child, Malekith.

-4419 Aenarion is slain at the Battle of the Isle of the Dead. Malekith is passed over as the new Phoenix King and Bel Shanaar is crowned in his place.

-4164 The foundation of the first colonies across the Great Ocean, lands later known to Men as the Old World. Malekith defeats the Orc warlord Gritok Redfang and saves the city of Athel Toralien.

-3997 Malekith fights alongside the Dwarf High King, Snorri Whitebeard, against a horde of Beastmen besieging Karaz-a-Karak.

-3419 Worship of the Underworld gods, the Cytharai, begins to spread in Nagarythe. Over the coming centuries these grow into dark cults that spring up across Ulthuan.

-2839 Malekith made ambassador to the Dwarfs.

-2789 Malekith begins his great period of exploring the world. In the northern wasteland he finds the Circlet of Iron in the ancient ruins of Vorshgar.

-2774 Malekith returns to Ulthuan to lead the war against the Cults of Excess and denounces his own mother as a traitor to the Elves.

-2751 The massacre at the Shrine of Asuryan. Malekith announces the suicide of Bel Shanaar and seeks the Phoenix Crown for himself. He is hideously burnt by the sacred flame of Asuryan.

Later that year a band of Naggarothi assassins attempts to slay Prince Imrik, chosen successor to Bel Shanaar, but are foiled by Chracian hunters. Civil war erupts across Ulthuan. Imrik passes through the flame of Asuryan to become the Phoenix King, taking the name Caledor.

-2749 The armies of Nagarythe occupy Tiranoc and much of Ellyrion. The eastern kingdoms hesitate, whilst Caledor I fights a series of desperate battles to stall the Naggarothi advances.

-2747 The Battle of Dark Fen. Naggarothi princes loyal to the Phoenix King fight against the army of Morathi and are defeated. They become exiles under the leadership of Alith Anar, the so-called Shadow King.

-2742 War breaks out in Saphery between mages loyal to Caledor I and wizards corrupted by the powers of darkness. The lands are desolated by their magical battles.

-2740 The Dark Elves, as the Naggarothi are now called, are pushed from the Inner Kingdoms back into Tiranoc and Nagarythe.

-2739 A renegade priest of Vaul, Hotek, steals the Hammer of Vaul from the shrine in Caledor and travels to Nagarythe. Sorcerers loyal to Nagarythe flee the Sapherian mages.

-2736 With the aid of the renegade Sapherians and Hotek, Malekith's Armour of Midnight is forged and the prince of Nagarythe becomes known as the Witch King.

-2735 Led by the Witch King atop the Black Dragon Sulekh, the Naggarothi armies push into the Inner Kingdoms once more.

-2724 Malekith and Caledor I finally meet upon the field at Maledor. Sulekh is slain and the Witch King is forced to retreat.

-2723 The Sundering. Malekith attempts to harness the power of Chaos trapped within the vortex of Ulthuan, to unleash an army of Daemons. The resultant catastrophe sinks most of the western isle, engulfing Nagarythe and Tiranoc beneath a tidal wave. The Naggarothi depart upon the Black Arks and travel north-west.

THE RISE OF NAGGAROTH

Dispossessed and vengeful, Malekith founded a new realm for his people – the dread land of Naggaroth from which the Dark Elves cast a shadow of terror upon the world.

The fleet of Malekith sailed westwards for many weeks, through driving rain, howling wind and waves like mountains that had been unleashed by Nagarythe and Tiranoc plunging into the ocean. Ever towards the sunset Malekith led his people – towards the dark and welcoming night. Across the Sea of Chill and the Sea of Malice the fleet travelled – two storm-wracked bodies of water that had claimed many Elven ships and their brave crews as they had attempted to explore the rugged coastlines of the western seas. In the uttermost westward reaches of the Sea of Malice, in the freezing shadows of the jagged Iron Mountains, the Black Arks of Nagarythe finally halted. Here, in this desolate land, Malekith declared he would recreate the glories of Aenarion's reign and build a capital to put the greatest cities of Ulthuan to shame.

The Founding of Naggarond

The Black Ark that had once been Malekith's castle beached itself upon the stony shore, fusing with the slate and iron-rich rocks of the foothills bordering the water. Food was scarce, though Malekith and his nobles led hunts across the foothills and brought back deer, boar and great shaggy mammoths to feast upon. Freezing winds howled down from the north, bringing snowstorms and chilling ice. More dangerous than the perils of frostbite and starvation were the many vicious predators that stalked these strange lands. The dark forests to the south and east, and the forbidding mountains to the west, held many fell beasts and hundreds of Naggarothi were devoured in the night as they made camps in the wilderness.

Scouts quickly found rich lodes of minerals in the mountains, but Malekith's people had no aptitude for mining and smelting, nor for building the walls that would be needed to keep away the mutant beasts, nor for farming or animal husbandry. They were warriors and most had known nothing but war – against Daemons, Orcs, Beastmen, and lastly against their fellow Elves. Malekith soon realised that although he still had a formidable fighting force, his people cared nothing for the building of a new civilisation. If the Druchii – the Dark Elves as their enemies had called them during the civil war – were to build a new kingdom in the west, they would need a work force to build it for them.

So began the bloodthirsty raids of the Dark Elves. At first, their attacks were directed solely against their kin in Ulthuan, to take food and other supplies. The High Elves for the most part would fight to the death rather than be taken in battle, and so Malekith's labour force did not grow quickly. Then word arrived from ships that had travelled further east, to the forests and mountains of the colonies where Malekith had once fought alongside the Dwarfs.

Primitive humans lived there, in caves and mud huts. They were brutal and stupid, but the Dark Elves did not care, for humans also bred quickly and were physically strong. Knowing that these short-lived savages could be easily controlled and swiftly grew in numbers, Malekith dispatched many fleets over the coming decades, to steal away whole settlements of humans and bring them back to Naggaroth.

GODS OF THE ELVES

The Elves worship a wide variety of deities of varying power and temperament. These beings are divided into two main spheres of influence, with neither having dominance over the other. This is encapsulated in the Elven belief of yenlui, or balance; a philosophy that dictates that there must be harmony between the light and dark natures of the Elven spirit.

The most widely acknowledged Elven gods outside of Naggaroth are the Cadai, or the gods of the Heavens, who represent the more positive characteristics of elven culture and the natural world. These are ruled by Asuryan, the greatest of the gods, and include such figures as Isha, goddess of fertility and healing, Kurnous the god of hunters, and Vaul the smith god.

In elven belief, many of the unsavoury aspects of their nature and the world at large are also represented by gods known as the Cytharai, or gods of the Underworld.

Of these, Khaine is the most well known, being a god of murder and war, but there are others such as Ereth Khial who rules the Underworld, Atharti, a goddess of pleasure and indulgence, and Hekarti the goddess of Dark Magic. These gods are not openly worshipped on Ulthuan, though they have small shrines that are usually shunned except during essential ceremonies of appeasement. Unlike their cousins on Ulthuan, the Dark Elves openly pay homage to these forbidding powers, the worship of whom rose through the Cults of Excess that preceded the civil war.

Though they understood little of what their lords asked of them, the humans learnt well enough from the whips of their masters how to dig ore from rock, herd cattle and forage in the woods. Guided by captured Elven masons and carpenters, the slaves began to build a city around Malekith's citadel. He named this place Naggarond, the City of Winter, and its dark spires started to tower higher and higher over the growing pirate port that nestled in its black shadow.

The Longest of Wars

With his capital established, Malekith turned his attention back to Ulthuan. Some of his people still clung to a pitiful existence in the ruins of Nagarythe, while the Blighted Isle, and upon it the Shrine of Khaine, was held by neither side. Though he feared to wield the Sword of Khaine himself, Malekith was well aware of its powers and the vengeance Caledor would wreak upon the Naggarothi should he claim it. To ensure that the Phoenix King did not claim the Godslayer, Malekith led an attack that swept across the northern isles of Ulthuan – the Shadowlands that remained of Nagarythe, what little had been spared by the tidal waves. The Elves of Ulthuan remembered the lessons of the civil war and Malekith was unable to forge across the mountains to attack the Inner Kingdoms. At sea, the burgeoning High Elf fleet grew bolder and reinforcements and supplies from Naggarond were often intercepted, further weakening Malekith's grip.

Caledor responded to Malekith's invasion with typical determination, ordering the construction of immense fortifications at each of the main passes through the Annulii Mountains. Never again would Malekith be allowed free passage to ransack and burn the shrines and cities around the Inner Sea. For thirty years Malekith probed and assaulted the outposts in the mountains, but Caledor's armies were well organised and disciplined and every attack was beaten back after vicious fighting. While their armies held back the sporadic raids and attacks of the Naggarothi, the High Elves completed the first of their citadels – Griffon Gate, which historians would later call the Unconquered Fortress. The other Great Gates of the Annulii followed in the coming years, and soon the passes between the sundered lands and the Inner Kingdoms were separated by ramparts hundreds of feet high, held by stalwart defenders, ingenious war machines and powerful spells of protection.

The Building of Ghrond

While Malekith fought upon Ulthuan, control of Naggaroth rested with his mother, Morathi. Now steeped in the blackest of magic, Morathi sought further means to increase her mystical power. She sent expeditions into the Realm of Chaos to the north, tasking them to seek out artefacts of the Dark Gods and to observe the ever-changing miasma of Chaos energy. Few of these expeditions returned, and none came back to Naggaroth unscathed. Too great were the perils for Morathi to venture there herself, and so she commanded a great tower to be built in the north of Naggaroth, from which she could personally look upon the energy of the gods.

Ghrond, the North Tower, this citadel was called, and here Morathi founded the Convent of Sorceresses. She set hideous tests of magical and mental strength to find the most promising young seers and witches from amongst the Dark Elves. Many did not survive; those that did were hardened by their trials, as bitter and devoted to the pursuit of black magic as their mistress. Morathi set this coven of Sorceresses to studying the Realms of Chaos, gazing into its mesmerising, mind-shredding depths to discern its secrets and learn of what had passed and would come to pass. With her dark oracles to aid her, the paths of the future were laid out before Morathi like an insane map, and with this knowledge she charted the course of destiny for her son. Yet for all her foresight and cunning, Morathi could not locate all of the strands of fate that would lead to ultimate victory over Ulthuan.

War in Ulthuan

The war at sea swung back and forth as much as the war on land, but after two hundred years of naval battles, the High Elves were gaining the upper hand. Their ships and crews were more disciplined than the bloodthirsty Corsairs of Naggaroth, who were used to raiding human and Orc settlements and fighting against unwitting and unsubtle opponents. The High Elves hit the Dark Elf convoys hard and then retreated, sapping the strength of Naggarond's fleet. Even the mighty Black Arks, once invincible, met their match. The *Palace of Joyous Oblivion*, commanded by Luthern

DURIATH HELBANE

Power and wealth are there for the taking; such is the creed of the Dark Elves. So it has been with Duriath Helbane, commander of the Black Ark Temple of Spite. In his seven hundred years as a Corsair, Duriath Helbane has raided cities of Ind, despoiled villages in the Southlands, fought ferocious lizards on the Dragon Isles and waged war against the armies of the Empire. His exploits have met with great success, yet he is still searching for the crowning glory to his career that will fix his name in legend.

To that end, Duriath has embarked upon an extremely hazardous yet potentially very profitable venture. He has assembled a fleet of more than two dozen ships and ten thousand Dark Elves. He has promised bloodshed and riches beyond compare to lure the bravest and most ferocious Corsairs to his cause. With this force he plans to invade the High Elf colonies in the Isles of Elithis.

Of course, there is a chance that he will meet his death in battle on those distant shores – or be cast astray by a storm, consumed by a sea monster or sunk by the fleets of the High Elves before he even reaches his target.

Yet Duriath Helbane, like those who follow him, is willing to dare anything for the prize that awaits them. If Duriath and his army can overthrow the effete rulers of the isles, he will burn their settlements to the ground and build a towering Dark Elf city in honour of the Helbanes. From here he will be able to control the routes from the Boiling Sea and have a virtual monopoly on the flow of exotic spoils to the courts of Naggaroth.

Fame, fortune and power await if Duriath is victorious – a worthy prize indeed!

Fellheart, was sunk by the enchanted starblade ram of the dragonship *Indraugnir* in a sea battle not far from the Blighted Isle. Their confidence shattered by this blow, the raiders of Naggaroth were more reluctant to dare the High Elf patrols over the coming years.

Though Malekith could make no inroads towards the Inner Kingdoms, his armies remained poised on the far side of the Annulii mountains, ever ready for a moment of weakness. The huge drain on the fleets and armies required to watch for Dark Elf attack seriously undermined the support Ulthuan could lend to the colonies across the other continents of the world. With the Inner Kingdoms secure against attack by the mountain fortresses, Caledor deemed the time was right to drive Malekith and his Dark Elves from Ulthuan once and for all. Once his borders were protected by the sea again he could then send vitally needed troops and ships to aid in battle all across the far-flung corners of the growing Elven empire.

For nearly ten years, the High Elf fleets sunk any Naggarothi ships that approached the northern coast. Their naval dominance was supreme, and the Dark Elves isolated on Ulthuan grew weary of their master's constant attacks against the impregnable fortress-gates of the Annulii passes. It was perhaps untimely, then, that Caledor chose to heap pressure upon Malekith by launching an offensive against the Shadowlands in a bid to claim the Blighted Isle.

Faced with this sudden aggression by their kin, the Dark Elves quickly set aside their seditious plotting and stopped their desertions, instead rallying to the banner of the Witch King. Fighting for their ancestral lands, the Naggarothi were hate-filled and vicious, and Caledor's advance swiftly stalled. Knowing that to retreat would be to give the Dark Elves an opportunity to counterattack, Caledor pushed onwards, fighting for every hillock, valley and isle. After a further ten years, the Dark Elves were finally driven from the Blighted Isle, at tremendous cost. Malekith's worst fear seemed at hand when Caledor travelled to the Shrine of Khaine. Yet for all the Witch King's dread, Caledor resisted the whispers of the God of Murder and left the Sword of Khaine in its black altar.

With the Blighted Isle now in High Elf hands, Caledor set sail to return to Lothern. His departure was seen by the scrying spells of Morathi and she called down a storm to sink the High Elf fleet. Most of the ships survived the battering wind and waves, but the fleet was scattered and Caledor's vessel was sent far off course. Guided by the sorcery of Morathi, Malekith's pirates swiftly intercepted and boarded the Phoenix King's ship. Knowing their intent was to capture him, Caledor cast himself into the sea in his full armour, escaping the torturous revenge Malekith had planned for him. Thus ended the reign of Caledor I, but his death did not end the war. Not for five thousand years have the Dark Elves known peace.

Hag Graef and Clar Karond

During the war, the Dark Elves had been defeated several times. Many of their commanders feared returning to Naggarond, wary of the Witch King's temper and the machinations of Morathi. They instead made landfall on the coast of the Sea of Malice many miles south of Naggarond, and here they built a city for themselves. The city was named Hag Graef, the Dark Crag.

Situated in a sheer-sided valley, the location of their new city was easily defensible against the creatures of the mountains and any punitive attack that Malekith might launch. An icy river that flows through the city to the Sea of Malice provided a natural harbour for Dark Elf fleets. Over the coming years, Hag Graef attracted other Dark Elves seeking to elude the Witch King for some real or perceived misdeed. Many of the raiders who travelled back from across the ocean first put in to Hag Graef, to unload a portion of their slaves and spoils before Malekith took his share. Sensing that this cauldron of dissent might prove rebellious in future years, Malekith at first thought to crush the dissidents and punish them for their insubordination. His hand was stayed by the intervention of Morathi, who had a far greater aptitude for subtle politics than her son.

Guided by Morathi's counsel, Malekith accepted this new city. He promised rule of the south coast of the Sea of Malice to the rulers of Hag Graef. An oath of fealty to the Witch King would ensure his protection. It was a masterful stroke, for the Dark Elf nobles of Hag Graef were soon gathering their power and took to fighting amongst themselves. Driven by their selfish ambitions, the rulers of Hag Graef looked to Malekith for favour, for they knew that the Witch King's support could tip the ongoing power struggle engulfing their city. Malekith invited half a dozen of the most powerful nobles of Hag Graef to a feast. He offered them a choice. One of the goblets of wine on the table, he told them, was poisoned. Any one of them willing to risk his life to rule should take a drink and Malekith would grant that noble a share of the city. Three of the nobles snatched up goblets without hesitation and downed their contents. They knew that it was better to be poisoned than suffer under the rule of the others. The last three, one-by-one, also drank, forced to prove their worth by the boldness of their peers. It was now that Malekith announced that in fact all of the wine was poisoned, and only by swearing unfailing loyalty to the Witch King would the princes receive the antidote.

The other princes who vied for control bargained with Malekith for warriors and sorcerers, and traded slaves and ships in return for his patronage. Caught up with their petty schemes, each of the ruling families eventually fell under the sway of Malekith, and only through the Witch King's patronage could they resist the ambitions of their opponents. In the end, they ruled only in name, for the Witch King had played them off against each other and now controlled them utterly.

From Hag Graef, the Dark Elves ventured into the Black Spine Mountains. Such expeditions were fraught with danger, as storms and marauding beasts took their toll.

For many years, it seemed as if the Dark Elves would be confined to the coast of the Sea of Malice, trapped between the bitter seas and the unforgiving mountains. This was to change dramatically when the Elves of Hag Graef mined further into the mountains. One day the slaves broke through a seam to find themselves in a huge subterranean chamber, many miles across.

A dark underworld sea glittered in the lantern light, fed by dozens of small streams from the heart of the mountains. As the Dark Elves pushed further into the mountains, they found a network of half-flooded caverns and tunnels that stretched the length of the mountain chain. Many were natural formations, while some had the disturbing look of having been hewn by mortal hands in ages past. The caverns were not deserted; all manner of strange animals made their homes in the dark beneath the world. The Dark Elves found other entrances and built fortified gates from which to launch expeditions and guard against monsters rampaging into their lands.

To the east, a group of Dark Elves founded the city of Clar Karond, linked to Naggarond and Hag Graef by underground tunnels. Particularly in the freezing winter months, travelling under the surface proved much safer than overland or across the storm-wracked Sea of Malice. Clar Karond quickly grew in size and importance, as its location further east made it a natural port for returning Corsair ships. From Clar Karond, slaves and other prizes were moved swiftly to the mines of Hag Graef or to the capital. It saved weeks of sailing for ships to be sent out on raids from Clar Karond, and Malekith ordered a shipyard to be built there. Within twenty years, more ships came and went from Clar Karond than Naggarond and Hag Graef combined. The chance to profit from this endeavour was not missed by Malekith, who again pitted the strongest noble families against each other with the promise of controlling this lucrative trade.

The Cult of Khaine Grows

While Clar Karond prospered, politics and infighting became rife within Naggarond. Remnants of the many pleasure cults from Ulthuan continued to hold sway over the Dark Elves, but one sect in particular rose to dominate all others. They were cultists of Khaine, the God of Murder, and their bloody sacrifices made a great spectacle for the Dark Elves. The fumes from their pyres swathed the city of the Witch King, and bloodthirsty mobs ran rampant through the streets, killing and maiming in mindless bursts of violence. Rather than quell these excesses, Malekith sought to focus the devotion of these Elves and turn it to his own ends. The Witch King proclaimed himself a mortal incarnation of Khaine, his merciless instrument in the realm of the living. Malekith swore undying devotion to the Lord of Murder in the shrine of Naggarond, and poured a goblet of his divine blood into the braziers where the Witch Elves burnt the hearts of their sacrifices.

Morathi again aided her son, and gifted the Witch Elves of Khaine with the sacred Cauldrons of Blood. The Hag Queens who led the cult bathed in the blood of their

them, while in the skies above winged creatures with iron skins and the heads of snakes soared amongst the unnatural storm clouds. The ragged horde filled the horizon with their numbers and they advanced south from the Chaos wastes as if the gods themselves chased them. The baying and roaring of their beasts could be heard for miles and the bitter cold did not slow nor turn their headlong attack.

To Ghrond came this Chaotic horde, and they fell upon the city in a headlong assault, crashing against the black walls like a frenzied tide. The repeater crossbows of the Dark Elves cut down hundreds of demented tribesmen, but they climbed over the hills of corpses to continually assail the ramparts of the North Tower. The Sorceresses sent mystical word to their mistress in Naggarond, though many were slain in the attempt by daemonic entities brought south upon the winds of Chaos.

For three weeks the siege continued, until at last the Witch King arrived with the army of Naggarond. The Black Guard led the relief, charging with their cruel halberds into the twisted Chaos-men and hacking them down. Spearmen drove the Chaos followers from the walls of Ghrond and allowed the defenders to sally forth and bolster the army of Malekith. Black-cloaked horsemen rode down those that tried to flee and hunted for survivors escaping across the barren tundra. Into the night the fighting continued, until not a single tribesman was left alive, though fully half of Malekith's warriors had also fallen. The Sorceresses that had survived were brought before Malekith; he had them thrown into chains and sent to the sacrificial altars for their failure to foretell the Chaos attack.

Strife in the Colonies

While the cities of the Dark Elves grew in Naggaroth, their exploits further afield also increased. In the new world across the oceans, where slaving fleets terrorised tribes of primitive humans, the influence of Ulthuan was growing ever stronger. High Elf fleets patrolled the coasts and made raiding more perilous year by year. Soon the slaves and spoils began to slow, and Malekith was most displeased. He ordered his Corsairs to target the Dwarf trade convoys, and provided maps of their secret routes that he had learnt whilst he was ambassador to Snorri Whitebeard.

The final part of Malekith's scheme was suggested by Khalaeth Mournweaver, ruler of Hag Graef at that time. The raiders went clothed as Elves of Ulthuan, swathed in white robes and silver armour brought back from raids on the Shadowlands. While they swelled the coffers of Naggarond, the Corsairs would sow dissent between the Elves and Dwarfs. Malekith laughed at the thought of the betrayal of both races that had once lauded him as a hero. The short, ugly Dwarfs and his effete kin on Ulthuan would never be able to unite against him.

The results of these clandestine attacks proved to be far greater than Malekith had ever hoped. Caledor II had succeeded Malekith's adversary during the civil war. Here was a Phoenix King who thought much of himself, and

sacrifices and rejuvenated their bodies, as did Morathi herself. Unlike Morathi, who kept the innermost secrets of the Cauldrons for herself, the Hag Queens' revivification was only temporary. As the months passed, they began to age once more and needed to bathe again to reclaim their beauty. For decades, the most powerful Witch Elves indulged themselves in this bloody manner, realising too late that Morathi had ensnared them with an addiction to eternal beauty. The Hag Queen Hellebron, leader of the cult, once refused her ritual bathing, but became so decrepit and age-worn that her loyal followers had to sustain her with their own blood until she repented and bathed in a Cauldron once more. She has been defiant of Morathi ever since, but ultimately it is Morathi who controls the fate of the Hag Queens, not Hellebron.

The Invasion of Chaos

It came about that as Malekith's reign as the Witch King neared its one-thousandth year, a great disturbance was seen within the Realms of Chaos. No seeress or sorcerer could discern what these storms foretold, but before long the intent of the Chaos Gods became all too clear.

From the north came a great host of savage humans riding upon vicious dogs and in war chariots drawn by giant predatory cats. Etched into their skin with scars and tattoos were symbols of the Dark Gods and pictograms of many-headed beasts. Misshapen Spawn and bloated beasts of Chaos ran and scuttled alongside

when the Dwarfs demanded explanation for the attacks on their merchants, his arrogance got the better of him. The stubbornness of the Dwarfs played its part also, and within three years, Ulthuan and the Dwarfs were at war with each other. When news reached Naggaroth of the growing conflict, Malekith rejoiced.

In celebration, he hosted a vast ceremony in Naggarond. The debauchery lasted for a whole month, and culminated in a massive hunt during which a thousand slaves were let loose into the forests and the Dark Elves chased them down over the following weeks. Calls for Malekith to lead his people back to Ulthuan became louder and louder, but the Witch King demanded patience from his subjects. The auspices cast by Morathi were good, but she warned that he must await the right time to strike.

For centuries the might of Ulthuan and the Dwarfs were pitched against each other. The Dark Elves profited greatly from the slaughter, roaming the coasts at will to strike wherever they wished. Their fleets waylaid ships packed with reinforcements as they were sent to the colonies, and raiding armies ambushed many Dwarf regiments as they marched along the coastal roads to attack the High Elves. As despair and death engulfed the realms of Dwarfs and Elves, the people of the Witch King prospered like never before.

In Naggaroth, Malekith's domains spread ever further. He gifted the city of Har Ganeth to Hellebron and her Khainite cultists. In return, the crazed Witch Elves would fight for the Witch King and his nobles when called upon. Har Ganeth became a thriving centre for the cult of sacrifice, and its bloody shrines rivalled those of Naggarond. In the centre of Har Ganeth Hellebron raised up a great temple, reached by an iron stairway of a thousand and one steps. At the top of the steps, the altars flowed with blood as sacrifices were made on an almost industrial scale.

Hundreds were slaughtered every day, beheaded by the chosen warriors of Khaine. The severed heads were tossed down the steps at the feet of which Dark Elves bit and clawed each other to grab the heads and take them home. From these blood-soaked rituals arose the cult of the Executioners – guards of the temple who became so gifted with their blades that they could decapitate or eviscerate a captive with one swift strike.

Malekith dispatched Assassins raised and trained in Har Ganeth, to sow disorder in the Elven colonies and Dwarf fortresses in the new world, to ensure that no accord could ever be reached between Elves and Dwarfs. Such measures were not needed, as Caledor II and High King Gotrek Starbreaker were now utterly committed to the destruction of each other.

Events finally took a turn that Malekith took to be the sign to attack. The Convent of Sorceresses spied a fleet leaving the port of Lothern, and aboard the flagship was the Phoenix King. He was departing Ulthuan to personally oversee the war with the Dwarfs. His garrisons had been all but stripped of fighters and his best generals lay dead in the colonies or had been disgraced and dismissed from court.

Malekith looked upon Ulthuan with eager eyes and saw that it was weak and vulnerable. He sent his riders to every city in Naggaroth, and recalled the greater part of the Naggarothi fleet. Every Black Ark returned to the Sea of Malice and an army the likes of which had not been seen for five centuries prepared for invasion. Malekith was confident that, divided and leaderless, Ulthuan would not resist him this time.

Anlec Rebuilt

As the Dark Elf Armada crossed the Sea of Chill, ships from the east brought news that might bode well or ill for Malekith's invasion. Caledor II was dead, slain by High King Gotrek Starbreaker. The Witch King had not expected such a turn of events and his thoughts shifted to who might be named as successor to the Phoenix Throne. With the incompetent Caledor II ruling Ulthuan, Malekith had been confident of overwhelming his kinfolk in a lightning campaign. If another king with the steel of Caledor I were chosen, such a swift victory would be impossible. Malekith resolved to take matters into his own hands and ordered the fleet to make all speed to the coast of the Shadowlands. If the Dark Elves attacked before a new Phoenix King could be chosen, they would be able to use the confusion and disarray to secure victory.

The Black Arks *Citadel of Ecstatic Damnation* and *Jade Palace of Pain* beached amidst the ruins of Nagarythe. Malekith had chosen his landing site well, amongst the overgrown fortifications of ancient Anlec. He would build Anlec anew and from the lands of the great Aenarion would strike out to reclaim his rightful rulership of Ulthuan. With many thousands of slaves labouring beneath the cruel whips of the overseers, the ramparts and bastions of Anlec were built again around the foundations of the Black Arks. Upon the site of Aenarion's throne room, Malekith raised his flag in proclamation to Ulthuan that Aenarion's heir had returned. As slaves began to erect a new palace to the glory of the Witch King, the Dark Elves moved south and besieged Griffon Gate, beyond which were the verdant Inner Kingdoms.

Faced with imminent war, the princes of Ulthuan swiftly chose their new king. Caradryel, Prince of Yvresse, was elected as the most stable of the candidates, and his first decree was to recall all loyal Elves to defend Ulthuan. Thus it was that the Elves left the lands across the sea, and they did not return for many centuries. Their wars and labours would remain unseen by the wider world. As reinforcements rushed back to Ulthuan, Malekith threw the might of his army against the sparse defenders of Griffon Gate. For all the strength of the Naggarothi host, such was the cunning artifice of the defences and the resolution of the High Elves that Malekith's army could make no headway and the siege ground on for many years.

As Elves from across the globe returned at Caradryel's call, the Phoenix King instituted a system of rotating garrisons that ensured that the gates across the Annulii Mountains were always defended at full strength. The Dark Elves could afford no such strategy and were tired and demoralised, while their enemies ever seemed fresh and prepared. Yet for all the steely resistance of his people, Caradryel had sacrificed many of the colonies abroad and the power of the High Elves slowly diminished with the shrinking of their empire. In the cracked and cratered remnants of Nagarythe, Anlec grew ever larger as the Witch King moved more and more of his people back to Ulthuan, until the cities of Naggaroth were empty except for the slaves and their keepers. All of Malekith's will and energy was bent on breaching the defences of Ulthuan.

Caradryel was no soldier, but the war with the Dwarfs had given rise to many great leaders and it was to these Elves that the Phoenix King gave command of his armies. Of these, the most gifted was Tethlis. His experience at war was equalled only by his hatred of the Dark Elves, who had left him an orphan after one of their many raids. Tethlis had been one of the generals discarded by the arrogance of Caledor II, but Caradryel put his faith in the coldly determined commander. He tasked Tethlis with driving the kin of Naggaroth back from the walls of Griffon Gate. Tethlis accepted this command with grim enthusiasm and from the various gate garrisons he mustered the most deadly veterans into a single army with which he would cast the Dark Elves back into the sea.

The High Elves' offensive was utterly unexpected, as a column of glittering knights charged from Griffon Gate and Dragon riders soared overhead. The Witch King had left the siege to his lieutenants, and the Dark Elves fled before the fury of Tethlis' attack. Northwards Tethlis drove the Naggarothi host, harrying them constantly, allowing them no respite to recover their nerve and choose their ground. When news of the rout reached Malekith he flew into a rage, tearing the head from one of the messengers and hurling it at his fellow heralds. Gathering his most fell warriors – Assassins of Khaine, Sorceresses of the Convent and battle-hardened Corsairs – Malekith marched out to meet the host of Tethlis.

He now had a new weapon to unleash upon the Elves of Ulthuan. The Witch King rode upon a massive chariot wrought from black iron and enchanted with spells of dread and destruction. Two vicious reptiles pulled it, Cold Ones found in the undercaves of Naggaroth. Behind Malekith, those nobles who had proven their dedication advanced. Some rode in other chariots, others upon the backs of yet more Cold Ones. The High Elves had never seen such creatures in great numbers before. Faced with the ferocious assault of the foul-smelling beasts, spearmen and archers fell back in disarray before the Dark Elf charge. Though the reverse was unexpected, Tethlis had not plunged foolishly headlong towards Anlec. He brought up reserves of White Lions and Phoenix Guard, and the High Elves rallied and retreated in good order behind the ranks of these deadly warriors. For all of Tethlis' cold fury, the Dark Elves had retained a foothold on Ulthuan and the Blighted Isle.

Rise of the Slayer

Despite the best efforts of Malekith's assassins to hasten his demise, Caradryel reigned for just over six centuries, during which Malekith continually tested the defences of Ulthuan. After Caradryel died peacefully in his bed, Malekith's spies returned from the Inner Kingdoms to bring word that the council of princes had elected Tethlis as his successor. The Witch King knew this did not bode well for his desire to claim Ulthuan. Tethlis had the tenacity and military verve of Caledor I, who had thwarted Malekith's ambitions so many years before. He fully expected Tethlis to resume his campaign against Anlec and so Malekith drew his forces back to protect his new capital. Within a decade, the High Elves came again, launching attacks from the Annulii Gates to strike into the heart of the Shadowlands.

The armies of Tethlis were more disciplined and coordinated than any force had ever been. Now formally trained in their towns and cities, these warriors fought for their homes and out of love for their king. Malekith's warriors battled bitterly, out of hatred for their cousins and fear of their lord. Such bloody battles had not been seen since the civil war. Within forty years Tethlis' offensive, which would be recorded in High Elf annals as the Scouring, threatened to push the Dark Elves out of Ulthuan altogether. Malekith struck back with ferocious counter-attacks and twice was forced to face Tethlis outside the gates of Anlec itself. On the second occasion, Malekith drove his warriors onward in a vicious pursuit, dogging the steps of Tethlis all the way to the Griffon Gate.

Sensing the fortress was poorly defended, Tethlis' army having been scattered by the implacable pursuit, the Witch King ordered an immediate assault. Malekith was to be outdone, however, as Tethlis' whole attack and flight had been feigned – a lure to bait the Witch King from his fortress. As the Dark Elves stormed towards the gates, bolt throwers and archers on the valley tops unleashed a storm of arrows that slew one in five of the attackers in the first volley. Tethlis' army regrouped according to the Phoenix King's plan and cut off the Witch King's escape from the pass.

The High Elves were overwhelmed by the first attacks. Several fortresses fell within the first month and isolated garrisons were slaughtered or taken captive. Such was the surprise that Tethlis had no time to mobilise his armies, especially in the depths of winter. The Dark Elves swept through Phoenix Gate and Dragon Gate. However, the success of Malekith's armies proved to be their undoing. They pressed on into the Inner Kingdoms where the weather was much milder. Here Tethlis' hosts awaited them, and they had emptied the winter stores of all food and razed their own villages to deny the Dark Elves shelter. Even the magic of Morathi and her Sorceresses could not protect the armies from the pangs of hunger and thirst, and supplies ran incredibly low. Knowing that to fail was to invite disaster, the High Elves sold their lives dearly.

Such bitter fighting came to a head at the Siege of Tor Lehan. So determined were both sides not to retreat that they wiped each other out – not a single High Elf or Dark Elf survived the siege. Tor Lehan marked the high point of the Dark Elves' advance. As winter abated, more troops were ferried across the Inner Sea from the eastern realms and the Dark Elves were soon outnumbered. They were within a few days' march of the Shrine of Asuryan but their attack could go no further. Hatred of their kin and fear of their king had driven the Dark Elves this far, but it could drive them no further. With the advantage of surprise well and truly gone, the Dark Elves' morale collapsed. They knew that to stay in the Inner Kingdoms was to risk their enemies surrounding them. Malekith's commanders ordered the retreat to Nagarythe.

The Blighted Isle Falls

Malekith's bloody recriminations were short-lived as Tethlis launched his inevitable counter-attack. For all his guile and sorcerous power, there was nothing the Witch King could do to halt the tide of High Elves pouring into Nagarythe. He abandoned Anlec, breaking out of a siege that lasted for two hundred days, and made for the sanctuary of the Blighted Isle. Left empty, mighty Anlec was destroyed by Tethlis' army; razed from existence by blade, fire and magic. Even the stones from which it was built were melted or ground down so that no trace of Anlec remained to stain the lands of Ulthuan. At the centre of the palaces had stood an Altar of Khaine, which had claimed so many Elf lives their spirits could be heard screaming in torment around its baleful stone. The altar and the earth beneath it, saturated with the blood of so many sacrifices, were dug from the ground and taken out to sea, where they were dropped into an undersea chasm. To this day, the shrieks of the Witch King's victims haunt the waves of that coast, terrifying sailors who dare cross those seas.

Still not content with driving the Witch King and his armies from the mainland of Ulthuan, Tethlis pressed onwards to the Blighted Isle. An armada of hundreds of ships left the shores of the Elven isle to face a dozen Black Arks under the command of Menreith Fellheart, grandson to the lord of the *Palace of Joyous Oblivion* that had been sunk so many centuries earlier. Menreith was determined not to suffer the same fate as his forefather, and the Battle of the Waves is remembered

Only the sheer viciousness of the Witch Elves and Executioners of Khaine leading the breakout allowed the Dark Elves to hack their way free. As he led the remnants of his army northwards again, Malekith cursed Tethlis' name and vowed to see the Phoenix King dead.

The war continued for another hundred and fifty years, during which Assassins and agents of Malekith tried several times to kill Tethlis. They came closest to success when they caught Tethlis travelling north from the Phoenix Gate. His bodyguard of White Lions was small, but they fought to the last Elf to defend their king, whose own blade accounted for half a dozen of his attackers. Though his guards were all killed, Tethlis himself suffered not a single scratch and he returned to the Phoenix Gate unharmed

Over the two hundred and fifty years since his ascension to the Phoenix Throne, Tethlis had waged war upon his dark cousins, and now the army of the High Elves was ready for the final push. Forewarned by Morathi's daemonic messengers, Malekith chose to strike first, before the weight of Ulthuan's hosts could fall upon Anlec a final time. Bitter winter snows and winds swathed Nagarythe and Tethlis' army was forced to retreat to the gates and would be unable to launch their campaign until the following spring. Shrouding his army in sorceries that warded away the winter chill, Malekith sent forth his remaining legions. Their orders were simple: take the Inner Kingdoms or die at the hands of the Witch King and his torturers.

as one of the most closely fought and bitter naval battles between the two races of Elves. Despite the power of the Black Arks, Menreith could not prevent the forces of Tethlis making landfall upon the Blighted Isle. The High Elves were greeted by a hail of crossbow bolts that scythed though Tethlis' troops as they disembarked into the shallow surf. Bodies and blood littered the waters as the volleys poured down from the cliff tops into the seas below.

Sharks sensed the blood in the water and gathered to feast on the dead and the living alike. Uncaring of the dangers, driven on by hatred of their kin and desperation to protect their final foothold in Ulthuan, the Dark Elves charged into the waters. Amidst the thrashing of the sharks, engulfed by waves and the screams of the wounded, the High Elves and Dark Elves butchered each other, fighting up to their waists in water, hacking at each other with primal fury. With the dead choking the red waters, the High Elves battled their way onto the land.

The bolts from the crossbows on the cliffs were relentless, hitting friend as often as foe, for the warriors of Malekith knew only that they had to drive their enemies back into the seas where the Black Arks awaited them. Unbeknownst to the Dark Elves, Tethlis had dispatched a small group of Hawkships from his main fleet, each with a mage aboard to swathe their vessel in a fog that obscured all detection. This flanking force beached upon the Blighted Isle several miles south of the main landing and from their holds rode dozens of Silver Helm Knights, assembled from the most powerful noble families in Ulthuan. The cavalry raced swiftly along the shoreline and fell upon the rear of the Dark Elves holding the cliffs. Swept away by the thunderous charge of the Silver Helms, many of the Dark Elves were driven over the cliff tops and fell to a hideous death on the jagged rocks below.

With their beachhead secure, the High Elves pushed more troops onto the Blighted Isle and advanced upon the Shrine of Khaine. Most of Malekith's warriors were still aboard the Black Arks and could not intervene. Sensing that not even his personal attention could hold back Tethlis' vengeful advance, Malekith quit the Blighted Isle on the back of a Manticore and sent word that his fleet was to return to Naggaroth.

The Blighted Isle had been lost, and with it all Dark Elf presence had been driven from Ulthuan. Malekith knew the temper of Tethlis and predicted that the Phoenix King would not be content while the Witch King still lived. Hidden from the eyes and spells of the High Elves, a cabal of Assassins lay in ambush around the

Shrine of Khaine. If Tethlis attempted to draw the Widowmaker, they would strike at once, cursed to sell their lives to prevent the Phoenix King from drawing the Murderer of Gods. None in Naggaroth know for sure what befell Tethlis as he stood before the black altar of Khaine. He was heard of no more, and it seems likely that Malekith's Assassins succeeded in their attack. Yet, whispered rumours persist to this day that the Witch King's killers were slain by the White Lions who guarded Tethlis, and that it was the bodyguards themselves who slew the Phoenix King when he tried to take the Sword of Khaine; an act that would have plunged all of the Elves into a new age of darkness and bloodshed to rival the times of Aenarion.

Whether by the hand of foe or friend, Tethlis died at the Shrine of Khaine, and with him the last remaining desire for war was quenched. The High Elves had burnt their own lands and seen their people slaughtered in the fight against the Dark Elves, and they had no more stomach for battle. For his part, Malekith knew his armies were broken, their fighting spirit spent upon a thousand fields of battle, and the Dark Elves returned to Naggaroth to rebuild their strength.

The Age of Hateful Peace

Exhausted by centuries of war, both the High Elves and Dark Elves had spent the last of their strength during the Scouring. In Naggaroth, the survivors of the war drifted back to their homes, quiet and chastened by defeat. Even the all-night sacrifices ordered by Hellebron and the hunts organised by the Witch King could do little to lift the morale of the Dark Elves. The fleet commanders willing to dare the High Elf patrols to the east were few and raiding ships slipped away and returned as sole hunters, unable to gather in great strength and repeat the mighty invasions of the past. Knowing that his people needed time to revive their spirits, and wary of any threat that might prove the fatal blow to their wounded pride and lead to uprising, the Witch King turned all his resources to rebuilding the strength of Naggaroth and its six cities. He instigated the construction of a chain of fortified towers along the border with the Chaos Wastes, to aid Ghrond in its eternal vigilance. He stationed three Black Arks in the Dire Straits, the perilous stretch of water that led from the Great Ocean to the Sea of Chill, to protect against any High Elf incursion.

It was not long before news began to spread across Naggaroth that cheered the cold hearts of the Dark Elves and stirred in them their old desire for slaughter and mayhem. Kaledor Maglen, famed lord of the Shades and greatest explorer of the Underworld, had discovered a passage to the west, into the Boiling Sea. Named the Black Way for its miles of lightless tunnels, this new route would allow the fleets of Naggaroth to pass into the west and avoid the armada of Ulthuan. In the Boiling Sea, the Black Arks found monstrous creatures, and Beastmasters from Karond Kar shackled these titanic monsters and broke them to the will of the Dark Elves. With spired castles upon their backs, the serpentine creatures of the Boiling Sea became the core of a new raiding fleet.

The construction of the northern watchtowers was completed, and not too soon, for Chaos warbands began to gather in the Chaos Wastes and foray into the lands of Naggaroth. Patrols from the fortifications swept the lands clear of the primitive human tribes that came south intent on pillaging; all that they found was a grisly death or the chains of the slavemasters.

For all his intent on rebuilding the power of the Dark Elves, Malekith never turned his gaze from the ultimate prize: Ulthuan. Spies and agents he had there still, while the auguries of Morathi and her Dark Convent provided the Witch King with much information. A wave of intellectual endeavour had swept the isle of the Elves, following the rise to power of Bel-Korhadris, a mage of Saphery. The mage-king built a great edifice to his own glory and the study of the magical arts, raising the White Tower of Hoeth to rival the soaring spires of Ghrond. The Witch King sensed a growing weakness in the heart of the High Elves, a softening of their souls as

generations passed and the bloody battles of the Scouring slipped from living memory. But not for him would those bitter conflicts be forgotten, for Malekith was now so steeped in Dark Magic he did not age, and his people were forever reminded of their duty to their lord and the wrongs that had been done to them.

The Silent War

Direct war against the High Elves would serve no purpose, Malekith realised. Outright aggression would only stir them from their introverted decline, while the Witch King could use more subtle means to defeat his foes from within. Advised by Morathi, Malekith poured support into the many cults and sects that the Dark Elves participated in, openly supporting High Priests and High Priestesses like Hellebron, Aegethir and Kherathi. The cults' ceremonies became ever more extravagant and widely attended.

Luxuries were heaped upon the most dedicated followers of the Dark Elves' sinister gods. From amongst the ranks of these fervent worshippers, the Witch King selected the most intelligent and devoted, and they were sent to learn the arts of subterfuge and spying from the Assassins of Khaine. When they were ready, these agents travelled, one at a time by hidden routes, to the shores of Ulthuan. They blended in with the High Elves and assumed normal lives as carpenters and smiths, as farmers and poets. All the while, they began to spread their poisonous beliefs, and the ancient cults of pleasure began to grow again. This time the cults were insidious and subtle, daring none of the flamboyant rituals that had exposed them in the time of Bel Shanaar. Century by century, generation by generation, the hidden sects flourished; a dark canker at the heart of Ulthuan that remained unseen by those who reigned.

When Aethis succeeded Bel-Korhadris as Phoenix King, Malekith knew that the time had arrived to unleash his hidden agents. Aethis was a weak-willed aesthetic. Under his reign the arts rose in prominence, and under the cover of this the cults created by Malekith expanded swiftly and struck without warning. Kidnappings and murders blighted the cities of Ulthuan. Terror of this unseen foe gripped the land, paralysing the High Elves. Nobles were found slain in their beds, mages disappeared from their towers and children vanished from their classrooms. Panic swept through Ulthuan as these crimes grew in boldness and horror, until Aethis finally acted.

Although Malekith's cultists were wreaking havoc, they were not unopposed. When Bel-Korhadris had built the White Tower of Hoeth he founded a company of mystical guardians to protect it – the Swordmasters. Unknown to either the Phoenix King or Malekith, the Swordmasters were waging a silent war against the pleasure cults and the conflict came to a climax in Lothern itself, when fighting erupted on the streets of the city between Naggarothi agents and the warriors of the Swordmasters, during which the cultists were all slain. Forced to abandon some of their bolder plans by the persecution of the Swordmasters, the cults of excess faded back into

High Elf society and continued their secretive work. Even as cultists were uncovered and executed, more agents were dispatched from Naggaroth to swell the ranks of the cults. Some of these were discovered and slain as soon as they landed on the coast, others slipped through the guard of the High Elves and established themselves as their predecessors had done.

This centuries-long infiltration reached fruition when Girathon, one of Malekith's most trusted agents, acquired the position of chancellor to the Phoenix King. Girathon used his power to subvert much of Aethis' commands and spread confusion throughout the realm. When his loyalties were uncovered, Girathon assassinated the Phoenix King before he was himself slain. Malekith ordered a parade and three days of bloodletting in gratitude to the slain agent. What made Girathon's death all the more remarkable was its utter falsehood. Girathon had long been the Witch King's spymaster and when he became directly involved with the Phoenix King, he engineered his own capture and the subsequent opportunity to strike down Aethis.

Fleeing retribution, Girathon swapped places with an innocent servant of the court, casting a glamour upon his victim to give him the appearance of the spymaster. It was this unwitting pawn who was tortured to death, still raving his innocence, while Girathon commandeered a Hawkship from the harbour and led its crew into a Dark Elf ambush a few miles out to sea.

Girathon continued to serve the Witch King for another three hundred years, during which he returned to Ulthuan eight more times. He had faked his own death so that he could continue to operate within Naggaroth and Ulthuan in absolute secrecy. His personal joy was acts of sabotage, always carried out in such a way that they left evidence pointing to an innocent Elf, who would then be executed for the treacherous acts. Eventually, Girathon's natural talent for schemes and politics caught up with him – he finally died at the hands of his master when the Witch King learnt of a plot by Girathon to seize control of Ghrond.

The Day of Blood
In the coming years, rule of Ulthuan passed to Morvael, known in history as the Impetuous. Outraged by the actions of Malekith's agents, Morvael gathered a war fleet and sent it to Naggaroth to exact revenge for the murder of Aethis. The Sorceresses of Ghrond sent warning, having foreseen the High Elves' assault in signs from the Realm of Chaos. The Dark Elves were ready for the attack and the High Elf host was soundly defeated as it landed its troops. The Dark Elves fought savagely and the massacre is celebrated as the Day of Blood. More than half the High Elf fleet was destroyed and sensing weakness in Ulthuan's defences, Malekith did not hesitate to send out the call to arms, launching his hosts and fleets upon Ulthuan once more.

As before, Anlec became the foundation of the Dark Elves' occupation and was rebuilt over the course of a decade using iron-hard black stone from the quarries of Naggaroth. Though lacking the sheer size and grandeur of its previous incarnations, this new Anlec was still a formidable fortress and a secure base from which Dark Elf armies once more besieged Griffon Gate.

With so many warriors lost in the attack on Naggaroth, Morvael was forced to institute a system of militia levies on the people of Ulthuan, insisting that all Elves be trained for military service. When news reached Malekith of this development, he scorned these new troops, dubbing them cowardly bakers and farmers. The first few levies fared badly against the vicious and battle hardened warriors of Naggaroth, but their presence ensured that Griffon Gate was always defended over the next thirteen years. Malekith believed that the quality of his troops and the power of his Sorceresses would eventually prove too much for the garrison, and that it would be only a matter of time before the fortress fell to the army of the Witch King.

Malekith had another reason to be confident. He was using his magic to visit nightmares upon the Phoenix King, testing his sanity with visions of Ulthuan engulfed in flames and Morvael's family lanced upon spikes amidst the ruins of the White Tower of Hoeth. Season-by-season, the dreams inflicted upon Morvael became darker and ever more disturbing, turning the Phoenix King into a nervous, gibbering wreck.

Fighting against madness and driven by a heartfelt paranoia, Morvael emptied the Phoenix King's treasuries to rebuild the High Elf fleet. Resurgent again, the warships of the High Elves attacked the supply routes from Naggaroth to Anlec, cutting off Malekith from fresh warriors, food and weapons. While the battles at sea raged, Mentheus of Caledor, a renowned general, took matters into his own hands. Mentheus gathered together an army in a desperate attempt to relieve the siege at Griffon Gate. With a host of levy spearmen, mainly from Chrace and Cothique, Mentheus marched to Griffon Gate, accompanied by a cadre of mages from the White Tower. Weakened by a lack of supplies, the army of Naggaroth was forced from the fortress by Mentheus' phalanxes of spears.

Over the following decades, sporadic fighting between the Dark Elves and High Elves erupted across the Shadowlands. Unable to muster the supplies for an outright battle, Malekith was forced to send his armies on hit-and-run attacks, luring Mentheus' forces into ambushes to whittle down their strength. Eventually, after more than three centuries of bloodshed, Mentheus' army succeeded in pushing back the hosts of the Witch King to the gates of Anlec itself. Here, the Dark Elves turned and faced Mentheus, determined that Anlec would never again fall.

The Witch King led his army from his black chariot, and the fighting raged for the better part of three weeks. In the final assault on Anlec, Mentheus was slain by a bolt thrower. His Dragon, Nightfang, went berserk and the

Dark Elves were scattered by the Dragon's rampage. The Dragon was eventually slain with dark spells, but by then Anlec was lost and Malekith was forced to quit Nagarythe once again, his bitterness and rage greater than ever.

The Witch King did have one final revenge. Driven mad by his dreams, overwhelmed by the terrors unleashed by the Dark Elves, Morvael committed suicide. In the Shrine of Asuryan, the Phoenix King abdicated and hurled himself in the sacred flames to perish. Seven Phoenix Kings had now died, and Malekith had seen them all pass, his life sustained by the dark energies of Chaos. The Witch King vowed that he would survive to see the last of the Phoenix Kings die, even if he had to wait another five thousand years.

Slaughter Across the World

For an age, the warriors of Naggaroth put aside their bloody wars with their kin on Ulthuan, to venture further and further abroad across the oceans. Driven by the urge to gather ever greater power, Dark Elf ship captains and glory-hungry princes set out across the oceans seeking plunder and adventure. Competition between the many family dynasties that held sway in the cities created inter-house rivalries that fuelled a massive expansion of the raiding fleets. Any Dark Elf with the right blend of determination, bravery and ruthlessness could make his or her fortune fighting on distant shores.

From the Boiling Sea, Black Arks could now raid the oriental lands of the farthest east. Yet for the Dark Elves these were uncharted territories and for each fleet that returned with prizes and slaves, half a dozen came back to Naggaroth in failure.

The most notable successes were by Laithikir Fellheart, latest in a long line of Black Ark commanders and as cunning a she-Elf as was ever born. Laithikir had learnt to follow the High Elf ships, her Black Ark swathed in shadow and storm, tracking their ever-increasing journeys to the lands of the orient. By shadowing the fleets of Ulthuan, she was able to raid the busy seaports and convoys that traded with the High Elves. As word of her success grew, Laithikir sold her charts to other captains, and within a decade dozens of Dark Elf fleets were attacking the settlements of the mysterious far east and bringing back tens of thousands of slaves and holds full of exotic wares such as witch jade, ivory, tigerfire, silk and spices. Ever-eager to show off their wealth and power, the Dark Elves prized these stolen wares highly and their value soared. Competition for the Witch King's permission to raid these lands fuelled a period of infighting and politicking that saw Malekith's coffers swell with gold and silver.

In the Temple of the Goddess of a Hundred Eyes, Corsairs crucified a hundred red-robed priests and took a dozen golden statues, which were presented to Morathi as a gift. The Black Ark *Citadel of Desolation*

sank untold fleets of unsuspecting nations and its raiders sacked entire cities. From hidden coves, Dark Elf raiders looted gold convoys and slave-traders, and brought back the riches of kings to adorn the palaces of Malekith.

At one unfortunate port, the Dark Elves encircled the town and barred all escape, before the Witch Elves were unleashed to wreak havoc within the walls. The Khainites named the town Khairith Irlean – the Place of a Thousand Bloody Delights. When the armies of the Dragon Emperor arrived, the Dark Elves had already returned to sea. In their wake, they left a town empty but for heaps of dismembered and charred corpses, writhing with flies and disease. The stones of the buildings were stained red with blood. So disturbing was the scene that the town was razed utterly and all mention of it was stricken from maps and records.

The Witch King himself once travelled to the farthest reaches of the world, and personally led many attacks. At one eastern capital, mystics called up strange illusions and beastly apparitions to assail the Dark Elves as they stormed the towers protecting the city. Malekith unleashed his own sorceries, driving the mystics insane and boiling the blood in their veins. The city was little more than a ruin when Malekith left, and as a last contemptuous act, he summoned up a great wave to drown the remains. The broken domes of shrines and the walled steps of the great pyramid temple still break the waves at low tide, an ominous reminder of the Witch King's power.

To the east, the sea patrols of the High Elves were sorely beset by ever-increasing raids by wild Norsemen and the raiding fleets of Naggaroth made great sport along the coasts of the Empire, Bretonnia, Estalia and Tilea. Shades from the *Tower of Oblivion* stole into the town of Anducci in Tilea's southern lands and crept into the houses of the local people, snatching all the children of the town from their beds. The commander of the *Tower of Oblivion*, Randelle Doomwhisper, then offered to ransom the children back to the townsfolk. After the terrified Tileans had gathered up all of their wealth and stores, the Dark Elves stormed ashore and slaughtered everybody. The captives were taken back to Naggaroth; to whatever unholy end none can say.

The Empire, for a time, had guarded its shores well, but division and civil war had split the people of Sigmar. In the confusion and anarchy of the following centuries, the Dark Elves found rich pickings. They even grew so

bold as to raid the port of Marienburg. Under the cover of night, the raiders unleashed a storm upon the city. Their Helldrakes glided effortlessly through the tossing seas and their crews cut out seven merchantmen from under the guns of Rijker's Isle, the port's keep. The Dark Elves unloaded what they wanted and then set fire to the ships and sent them back into the harbour, destroying dozens more vessels. By the light of the burning ships the Corsairs laughed and offered sacrifices to their evil gods and goddesses.

From beneath the Blackspine Mountains, the Dark Elves ventured further and further into Lustria to the south. They constantly assailed the High Elf settlement of Arnheim on the eastern coast of the New World and the city is now in a state of almost constant war.

Deeper into the ancient jungles, the Dark Elves discovered the soaring temples and hidden treasure vaults of the Slann and their Lizardmen servants. Laden with gold and strange artefacts, these expeditions were greeted with celebration upon their return. The raiders' tales of cities paved with gold and immense, prehistoric ziggurats filled with riches beyond counting lured more and more Dark Elves into the rotting jungles and raids into Lustria now take place every few years. For centuries the Lizardmen have launched retaliatory attacks against Naggaroth in attempts to retrieve their treasures, and the enmity between the two races remains particularly bloody.

THE TIME OF HATE

-2722 The Witch King founds the city of Naggarond upon the western shore of the Sea of Malice and creates the kingdom of Naggaroth. The Dark Elves begin to raid the shattered lands of Tiranoc for slaves to build their new city.

-2630 A Dark Elf expedition returns to Ulthuan and hostilities resume. Caledor reorganises the High Elf army for defence and begins the building of the gateway fortresses across the mountain passes of the Annulii.

-2600 Morathi creates the Convent of Sorceresses and construction begins on the great citadel of Ghrond.

-2425 The Dragonship Indraugnir, armed with a mighty starblade ram, sinks the Black Ark Palace of Oblivion near the Blighted Isle. This comes as a great blow to the Dark Elf fleet and marks the beginning of High Elf naval supremacy for many centuries to come.

-2343 The Dark Elves begin to explore the caverns beneath Hag Graef and discover the Underworld Sea. Many Dark Elves never return from the black depths. The caves and tunnels are found to stretch far beneath the Black Spine Mountains, and the first Cold Ones are captured and brought to the surface.

-2319 Dark Elf knights mounted on Cold Ones and chariots pulled by the reptilian beasts are used in battle for the first time, smashing a High Elf army. The Witch King rides to war atop the Black Chariot. Despite the impact of these new troops, the organisation and numbers of the High Elves prove insurmountable.

-2219 The High Elves finally succeed in pushing the Dark Elves from the northern coast of Ulthuan and begin to sweep the northern seas clear of Naggarothi ships.

-2200 The High Elves take the Blighted Isle. Morathi conjures a storm to isolate Caledor and his ship is attacked. The Phoenix King throws himself into the sea rather than be captured and taken to Naggarond.

-2201 Army commanders fearing for their lives after their defeat take refuge in the port of Hag Graef, which will eventually grow into a mighty city.

-2016 The city of Karond Kar is founded in the eastern wilderness of Naggaroth.

-2005 Attacks by Dark Elves disguised as their kin from Ulthuan further heighten growing tensions between the Elves and Dwarfs. Elven arrogance and Dwarfen stubbornness pitch the two races into a bitter war that lasts for centuries, exhausting the armies of both empires.

-1968 A group of sorcerers and sorceresses from Ghrond are shipwrecked upon the north coast of Nehekhara and are tortured by the priest Nagash until they teach him the secrets of Dark Magic. He eventually imprisons them within the Black Pyramid and goes on to become the Great Necromancer.

-1745 Har Ganeth becomes the centre of the cult of Khaine, ruled over by the Hag Queens.

-1666 A huge army of Chaos sweeps down from the wastes to besiege the citadel of Ghrond. The city holds out until the Witch King leads a relief force and defeats the savages at the Battle of Despair.

-1599 The Black Arks Citadel of Damnation and Jade Palace of Pain are beached upon the shattered isles of northern Ulthuan and Anlec is rebuilt. For the next hundred years the Dark Elves launch an invasion from Anlec that drives back the High Elves, but is held by the great gates of the mountains. Unable to breach the defences of the Inner Kingdoms, the Dark Elves tighten their grip on the northern lands.

-986 The Phoenix King Tethlis the Slayer commences the Scouring to drive every Dark Elf from Ulthuan.

-946 A Dark Elf counter-offensive reaches Griffon Gate but is wiped out in a trap. Dark Elf forces fall back to Anlec.

-922 A Dark Elf army is ambushed at the Battle of Grey Canyon while camped in a hidden valley of the Shadowlands.

-777 Dark Elf scouts trap Tethlis close to Phoenix Gate but the Phoenix King and his bodyguard fight their way free, slaying their attackers.

-732 The Witch King launches a devastating winter offensive, cloaking his soldiers against the cold with powerful spells. They take several High Elf fortresses, precipitating the bitterest fighting seen since the civil war.

-730 The siege of Tor Lehan, which sees both sides wiped out to the last Elf.

-696 The Dark Elves are driven from the shore and Anlec is destroyed.

-693 A great armada sails for the Blighted Isle and Naggaroth. The Battle of the Waves is fought on the Blighted Isle. The armada is forced to turn back. Tethlis dies in the Shrine of Khaine, his demise shrouded in mystery.

-238 Kaledor Maglen discovers the Black Way, a series of caverns in the Underworld Sea that lead westwards into the Boiling Sea. The Dark Elves capture Heldrakes and Sea Dragons and fashion new seacraft pulled by these monstrous beasts.

-87 Dark Elves begin to raid further westward towards Ind and Cathay.

176 Following incursions by growing numbers of Chaos warbands, Malekith begins to build a line of defensive watch towers on Naggaroth's northern border.

211 The watch towers are completed and almost immediately prove their worth when a Chaos army is spotted and destroyed before it can penetrate deep into Dark Elf territory.

499 Aethis the Poet becomes Phoenix King. The Witch King's agents in Ulthuan rekindle the cults of excess and begin to recruit members from the nobility.

753 Dark Elf ships raid far and wide across the globe, bringing back entire tribes and the populations of whole cities to labour in Naggaroth.

860 The Black Ark Talon of Agony is overturned and sunk by a gigantic magical tidal wave off the coast of Cathay.

1103 Laithikir Fellheart shadows High Elf fleets around Cathay and Nippon and begins a century of merciless raids that see the Fellheart family rise to great power. With her charts, other Dark Elf fleets maraud with much success along the rich coasts of Ind and Cathay.

1120 Posing as chancellor to the Phoenix King, Girathon assassinates Aethis and then escapes.

1122 A High Elf expedition sails to Naggaroth to avenge Aethis, but the attack is foreseen by the Sorceresses of Ghrond and annihilated by the Dark Elves as the forces try to land.

1125 The Dark Elves retaliate and invade the Shadowlands again. In a series of lightning battles, the High Elves are driven back until only scattered bands of Shadow Warriors inhabit the Sunken Lands. So begins a long guerrilla war between the descendants of Alith Anar and the Dark Elves.

1131 The Dark Elves rebuild Anlec once more.

1133 Griffon Gate is besieged by the Dark Elves. The Phoenix King Morvael appoints Mentheus of Caledor as his military commander. Citizen-militia are trained to keep the garrisons of the gates at full strength.

1134 Malekith begins to visit horrific nightmares upon Morvael, driving him ever deeper into paranoia.

1141 The siege of Griffon Gate continues. The fortress is surrounded by immense Dark Elf siegeworks and pounded by war machines and sorcery, but still holds against assault.

1146 A citizen army of spearmen led by the renowned general Mentheus eventually lifts the siege at Griffon Gate, overwhelming the weary Dark Elves with their numbers.

1502 Mentheus is slain as he assaults the Dark Elves at Anlec. Upon his death, Mentheus' Dragon goes berserk and routs the Dark Elves. Phoenix King Morvael, finally driven mad by the nightmares visited upon him by the Witch King, throws himself into the sacred flame of Asuryan and perishes.

THE WITCH KING'S VENGEANCE

With his power and glory restored, Malekith once more turned his vile attentions to the Phoenix Throne of Ulthuan, and launched a war that rages on to the present day.

As the Dark Elves extended their terrifying raids to the remotest regions of the world, the augurs of Ghrond began to see stark changes within the Realm of Chaos. The shifting inner energies of Chaos swelled with power, straining and boiling as they built up like a tide. Waves of despair and anger flowed through the miasmic vortices of raw magic, bringing scenes of death and destruction that both thrilled and chilled the onlookers. War was coming; Chaos was coming.

Such import was placed on these visions that Malekith and Morathi travelled to Ghrond to witness the unfolding scenes of slaughter and misery for themselves. Snow-swathed fields were awash with blood, strange onion-domed towns burned with magical fire and shambling, shapeless beasts fed on mountains of bloody flesh. Over and over the images emerged from the coruscating energies, each time a little different, a small detail or event somewhat changed as the flowing threads of fate intertwined and unravelled, changing the future.

Malekith sensed that dark times would soon be at hand and he would be ready to strike at the hated High Elves. With the power of Chaos strengthening, more tribes of northern Marauders tried to breach the cordon of the watch towers. The danger of invasion from the north vexed Malekith greatly, as he could not launch an invasion of Ulthuan while the borders of Naggaroth were unsafe. It was Morathi who turned consternation into opportunity. In a great caravan, a hundred laden wagons drawn by a thousand Cold Ones, the Hag Sorceress led an expedition into the north. With her she took ten thousand slaves, the riches of distant kings and a coterie of Sorceresses. Messengers were sent to the east and west, declaring that the Queen of the Elves would handsomely reward any who would fight for her.

The first tribe met Morathi with suspicion, but once they saw her cold beauty they were utterly bewitched. Pleasured by concubines and given gifts of gold, silver and gems, the chief of the tribe quickly swore an oath of fealty to the 'Elf Queen'. The same happened at the next encampment, and the next, and the next. As word spread, tribes travelled hundreds of leagues to seek out Morathi, and she created a palace of frozen ice and jet black rock to welcome her visitors. She lavished lustful attentions on the tribesmen and gave them jewellry and slaves. This continued for many months, until she had mustered a horde of tribesmen tens of thousands-strong. A year earlier, these vicious warriors had been intent on pillaging the cities of the Dark Elves; now they were pawns of Morathi ready to fight for the Witch King.

Slaves in the shipyards at Clar Karond laboured through bleak winter days and nights, building immense ships of timber and iron to carry the army of northmen – the Marauders were terrified of the Black Arks, and were too clumsy to sail upon the backs of Sea Dragons and Helldrakes. Guided by Dark Elf steersmen, this flotilla crossed the Sea of Malice to await its human cargo. West of Har Ganeth, the tribes gathered under the shadow of the Black Pillar – a towering shrine to the Chaos Gods carved from obsidian and studded with the skulls of sacrifices. From here they embarked upon their fleet and followed the Black Arks across the Sea of Chill.

The size and fury of the combined Dark Elf and Chaos attack swept aside all resistance. Black Arks beached across Nagarythe and the armies of darkness smashed through Phoenix Gate and Unicorn Gate. While the Marauders were left to burn and plunder as they saw fit, the vanguard of the Dark Elves speared into the woodland realm of Averlorn – the home of the Everqueen of Ulthuan. Malekith's aim was twofold: to sow panic and dismay with the Everqueen's death and to corrupt the powerful magic that she wielded. Though the Witch King's forces stormed through Averlorn and surrounded the camp of the Everqueen, she escaped with the aid of Prince Tyrion, who cut his way through the Dark Elves and fled with the Everqueen into the deep forests. The Dark Elves burnt Averlorn, razing woodland and meadow as they hunted for the Everqueen and her companion.

Elsewhere, the armies of Naggaroth advanced without pause, Malekith's generals eager to outdo their rivals. The Blighted Isle swiftly fell and once again the Naggarothi held the Altar of Khaine. In Ellyrion, the horsemasters sought to fight back, but the sorcery of Malekith destroyed their army and scattered the survivors. Dark Elf ships broke through Lothern into the Inner Seas, and victory was within Malekith's grasp.

While Ulthuan burned, the Witch King demanded that the Everqueen be found, or that her body be brought to him as proof of her death. Four Assassins of Khaine pledged their lives and souls to bringing Alarielle to Malekith and then set out on their quest. In the blasted lands of Averlorn, they played a deadly game of cat-and-mouse with the Everqueen and her guardian. Despite coming close on several occasions, the Dark Elves always found their prey had eluded them, but the net grew ever tighter.

Only at Lothern and the White Tower were the Dark Elf armies checked in their advance. Besieged, the desperate defenders held out, praying to the gods for salvation. Malekith gloried in the destruction and carnage and mercilessly crushed every army raised against him. He would strangle all hope from his enemies, and then finish them forever.

Yet a glimmer of hope remained for the High Elves, despite the darkness that had engulfed their lands. The Everqueen still lived, even if in hiding, and tales were heard of a young mage from Saphery who wielded magical power that was the match of the Witch King's sorcery. He brought down storms of lightning upon his foes and engulfed armies with conflagrations of white flame. He was Teclis, brother to Prince Tyrion, and soon Malekith and his followers would curse his name.

The Assassins seeking the Everqueen came upon their prey one night, almost by chance. Prince Tyrion fought with savage skill and defiance, and slew all four hunters. Yet with his dying breath, the last Assassin sent forth a daemonic familiar to bring word to the Witch King of the Everqueen's location. When the impish, bat-winged creature arrived in the camp of Malekith, the Witch King revealed his masterstroke. With unholy pacts of blood and depravity, Malekith had struck a bargain with a Greater Daemon of Slaanesh, a depraved and wicked creature called N'kari. In return for sacrifices and dark favours, N'kari would hunt down Alarielle and devour her soul. With chilling shrieks of joy, N'kari set off on the hunt, speeding through the charred forests of Averlorn in search of the Everqueen.

The Greater Daemon descended upon Tyrion and Alarielle in the last twilight hours of the night. For all his power and skill, Tyrion was wounded and easily smashed aside by N'kari. As the four-armed Daemon of Chaos loomed over the Everqueen, lightning suddenly erupted from the darkness, hurling N'kari back. In the starlight stood an emaciated figure, a sword wreathed in crackling magic in his hand. It was Teclis, Magelord of Saphery. With a bellow of hatred N'kari attacked, but a great coruscation of energy engulfed Teclis. At its touch, the shimmering sphere broke the magical aura binding N'kari to the world of mortals, casting it back into the Realms of Chaos. Feeling that his creature had been banished, Malekith howled with frustration.

The Battle of Finuval Plain

Enraged that Alarielle still lived, Malekith turned all of his fury upon the High Elves. The Witch Elves kept the fires of Khaine burning day and night, as they heaped captives by the hundreds onto the pyres. Ulthuan's rivers ran red with blood as wanton slaughter engulfed the isle. It seemed for all the world as if the High Elves would be obliterated by Malekith's vengeance.

In a final act of defiance, the army of Ulthuan drew what little strength remained at Finuval Plain. Here, High Elves from every kingdom and from beyond the seas were gathered to fight their last battle. The Witch King was unimpressed by the ragtag army of Tiranoc charioteers, Ellyrian cavalry, Sapherian mages and the weary militia regiments. From across Ulthuan, the hosts of the Witch King marched to Finuval Plain to crush the last resistance. The host of Malekith dwarfed that of the High Elves. Beastmasters goaded gigantic War Hydras into the battle line, while Witch Elves screamed obscene oaths to Khaine. Corsairs clad in cloaks made from the scales of Sea Dragons bared their wicked blades and hurled abuse at their hated enemies. Sorceresses and Hag Queens cavorted in dark rituals to summon their power. And beside Malekith stood Urian Poisonblade, the most deadly warrior to have ever been raised in Naggaroth.

The two armies clashed like a tide of black engulfing a white rock. Urian cut down a score of High Elves, seeking out Prince Tyrion, who in turn claimed dozens of Dark Elf lives with his runeblade, Sunfang. Malekith channelled ungodly energies to bring down fire and ruin upon his foes, whilst wrestling with the counterspells of Teclis. Daemons howled and gibbered as the titanic magical forces opened breaches into the Realm of Chaos, while upon the field Dark Elf and High Elf blood matted the grass and turned the ground into a crimson quagmire.

Seeing that the strength of Ulthuan could not prevail against the might of Naggaroth, Teclis sought to destroy the Witch King. The Elven Mage whispered a prayer to Asuryan and drew on the power of his staff, gifted to him by Alarielle. With all of his prayers behind it, Teclis unleashed a bolt of energy directly at the Witch King. Realising his peril, Malekith turned all his art and power to deflecting the deadly blast, but was too slow to divert it entirely. The bolt struck the Witch King and engulfed him with its energies. No ordinary spell, the magical blast awakened the vengeance of Asuryan that still lingered within Malekith's soul and had burnt within the breast of Malekith for nearly five thousand years. That wound of old, the hideous burning that would never leave him, raged anew through Malekith's body, searing his flesh and mind. Tormented by the god's judgement, Malekith summoned the last of his power and hurled himself into the Realms of Chaos to escape the crushing agony.

With their lord seemingly destroyed, the Dark Elves fled the wrath of Tyrion and Teclis, abandoning their armour and weapons in the speed of their flight. As news spread across Ulthuan, the High Elves rallied to the call while the Dark Elves melted away into the shadows and returned to their vessels. In Caledor great Dragons were roused from their slumber, while armies of High Elves marched to the relief of Hoeth and Lothern. While the northmen fought ignorantly against the resurgent High Elves, over the following years the Naggarothi slipped away with their spoils, back to their chill cities in the north.

Hatred Without End

Though Malekith was not slain by Teclis' spell, it seemed that he wandered the Realm of Chaos for an eternity. He has never spoken of what he endured, not even to his mother, but eventually Malekith clawed and fought his way back to the world of mortals and was found not far from the northern watch towers, his body broken, his armoured skin rent with savage gashes and dents. Morathi nursed her son for a year, pouring all of her vile magic and malice into his soul to revive him. In the ranting of waking nightmares, the Witch King spoke of castles of bones and forests of eyes. When he awoke from his fever, Malekith's eyes burnt with a new light. Gone was the raging anger, replaced now by a harsh coldness that pierces the soul of any who looked upon the Witch King.

For the last two hundred years Malekith has plotted, conspiring with seers and Daemons, seeking the time for his retaliation against Teclis and his kin. Bloated on their victory at Finuval Plain, the confidence of the High Elves grows strong, and their daring with it. An expedition led by Eltharion of Tor Yvresse attacked Naggarond itself – with stolen clothes Eltharion and a small group of warriors sneaked into the Witch King's capital and opened one of the gates for Eltharion's army to enter. Fires burnt as the High Elves ran amok, killing and razing what they could before stealing away into the pre-dawn shadows.

Where before Malekith would have flown into a berserk rage, now he calculates the demise of his enemies with chilling ruthlessness. His revenge against those who continue to defy him will be long and agonising. Now the Witch King sits within his chamber atop the highest pinnacle of Naggarond and gazes out upon the world. He senses great doom and death will soon come and he stands ready to unleash his legions once more.

THE TIME OF VENGEANCE

1783 An army led by Yrtain Nightwind assaults the High Elf colony of Arnheim in Lustria after Shades discover tunnels beneath the mountains and swamps protecting the northern approaches to the city.

1856 The Dark Elf Lord Maranith takes to the air mounted on the Black Dragon, Wrath. He attacks the fleets of Ulthuan from the *Black Ark* Fortress of Eternal Torture. Never bested in aerial combat, he slays several Dragon Princes above the waves of the great ocean. The High Elves name him Caledor's Bane and the title is carried by his deadly lance ever after.

1907 Lokhir Fellheart inherits command of the *Black Ark* Tower of Blessed Dread. *His first act is to have his father's officers sacrificed to the Dark Elf gods in return for their divine favour.*

1974 The Beastlord Rakarth leads an attack on the Bretonnian city of Brionne. War Hydras tear down the gates and the city is sacked.

1988 Soldiers from the Elector Count of Nordland's army find the coastal town of Debneitz in ruins, its inhabitants' flayed corpses nailed to nearby cliffs.

2005 An attempted assassination of Morathi is foiled. The Assassin dies before interrogation. Hellebron is suspected by the Hag Sorceress but nothing can be proven.

2087 Lokhir Fellheart butchers the priests of the Temple of Gilgadresh and has the Red Blades forged from looted statues.

2301 The Great Chaos Incursion. Morathi strikes bargains with the northern Marauders and turns their armies upon Ulthuan rather than Naggaroth. The Dark Elves invade the isle of the High Elves alongside the barbaric hordes. Malekith sends the Daemon N'kari to slay the Everqueen, but the Keeper of Secrets is defeated by Tyrion and Teclis. At Finuval Plain, Teclis unleashes the power of Asuryan against the Witch King, who casts himself into the Realm of Chaos to avoid death. Without their leader, the Dark Elves are defeated and driven from the Inner Kingdoms.

2303 The Dark Elves are finally pushed from Ulthuan after much bloody fighting.

2304 Morathi forges Heartrender in the fires of the Burning Mountain.

2307 The Assassin Gloreir leads a coterie of Dark Elf killers into Lothern to slay the Phoenix King, Finubar. The Phoenix King is saved by his White Lions bodyguard led by Korhil. A swirling battle takes place across the rooftops of the city.

2379 Corsairs from Karond Kar are shipwrecked close to the pirate isle of Sartosa. They steal several ships to escape and with the aid of local sellswords attack the cities of Luccini and Remas. They are betrayed by the mercenaries and enslaved by the pirate captains whose ships they had taken.

2387 Lokhir Fellheart raids the town of Tor Canabrae on the Ulthuan coast.

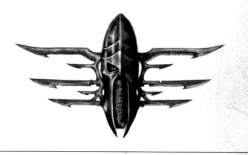

2402 A band of Shades sneaks ashore on the coast of Chrace, hiding out in the forests, raiding villages and ambushing patrols. It is a full year before a force of White Lions manages to bring them to battle, riding them down with their Lion Chariots. Nevertheless, a handful of the Dark Elves escape and are never found.

2416 Alondir Deathshard, Assassin Master of Har Ganeth, is slain by his best pupil, Shadowblade.

2418 The corpse of Ernezio Porcurio, mercenary captain of Luccini. is found inside a windowless basement beneath his castle, the cellar firmly locked from the inside. No trace of the killer is found.

2422 Lokhir Fellheart loots the sunken ruins of the Lizardmen city of Chupayotl and finds the Helm of the Kraken.

2423 Eltharion, son of Moranion, leads a daring raid against Naggarond itself. The Witch King swears revenge on his hated kin. He commands the ruling families to recruit fresh troops, appoints commanders from the most favoured lords, sends word to the raiding fleets to set sail, and launches a new invasion of Ulthuan.

NAGGAROTH

Chaos Wasteland

Ironfrost Glacier

Watch Towers

Watch Towers

Altar of
Ultimate Darkness

Ghrond

The Black
Pillar

Spiteful Peaks

Iron Mountains

Naggarond

Har Ganeth

Karond Kar

Sea
of
Chill

The
Monoliths

Sea
of
Malice

Hotek's
Column

Granite Hills

The Black Forests

Bear
Isle

The
Underway

Hex
Gate

The
Underway

Cold Water
Lakes

Hag Graef

The Gulf of Naggarond

Red
Desert

Lakes of
the Abyss

Doom
Gate

Pits of
Zardok

Clar Karond

Blackspine Mountains

Vaul's Anvil

Sewer
Gate

Maglen's Isle

Plain
of
Spiders

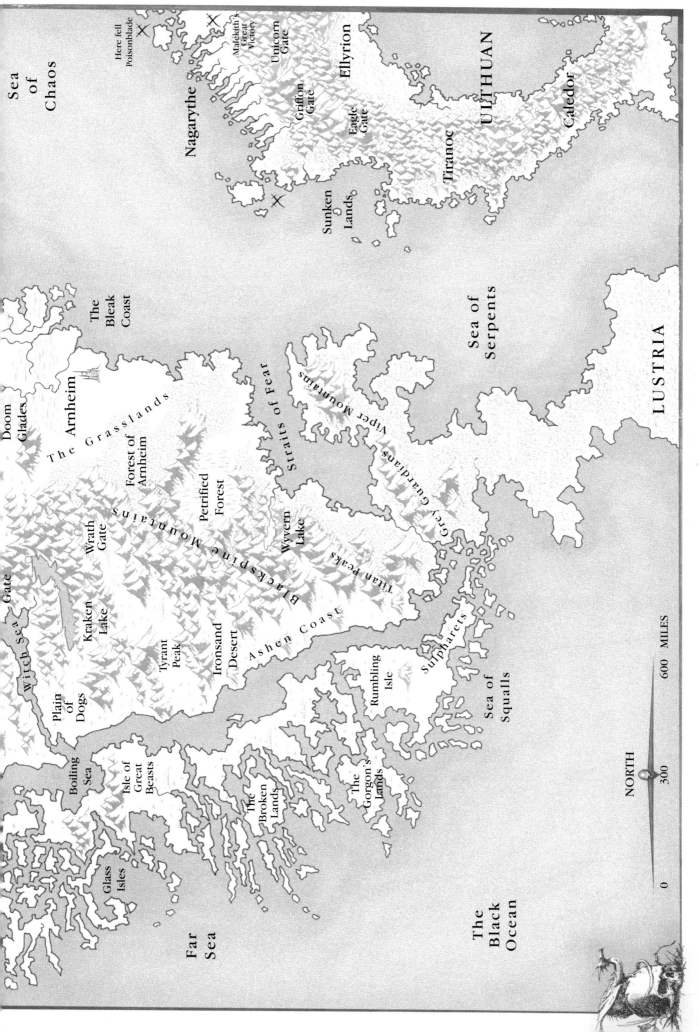

Sea of Chaos

Nagarythe

Here fell Poisonblade ✗

✗

✗ Malekith's Great Victory

Unicorn Gate

Ellyrion

Griffon Gate

Eagle Gate

✗

Sunken Lands

Tiranoc

ULTHUAN

Caledor

Doom Glades

The Bleak Coast

Arnheim

The Grasslands

Forest of Arnheim

Straits of Fear

Sea of Serpents

Witch Sea Gate

Wrath Gate

Petrified Forest

Viper Mountains

Grey Guardians

LUSTRIA

Kraken Lake

Blackspine Mountains

Wyvern Lake

Tyrant Peak

Titan Peaks

Plain of Dogs

Ironsand Desert

Ashen Coast

Boiling Sea

Rumbling Isle

Sulpharets

Isle of Great Beasts

The Broken Lands

Sea of Squalls

Glass Isles

The Gorgon's Lands

Far Sea

The Black Ocean

NORTH

0   300   600   MILES

REALM OF THE DARK ELVES

The lands of the Dark Elves are as harsh and unforgiving as their people. Sinister cities tower from the wind-swept tundra, casting their forbidding shadows across jagged mountains and shadowy forests.

The Dark Elves live in six heavily fortified cities, their innumerable towers built from black stone, rising like sinister pinnacles into the dark storm clouds. All of these cities are evil places, steeped in death and agony. Their lightless dungeons are crammed with captives whose wailings fill the air and whose moans seep through the thick walls of the high towers, saturating the soul with pain and misery. From the tips of the high towers, above the filth and smog of sacrificial fires, the Sorceresses cast their malign magic over the world.

The surrounding landscape is bleak and forbidding. To the north the land is flat, broken only by jutting outcrops of rock and scoured by gales. Black ribbons of rivers tainted by magic and blood criss-cross the ice fields, carving elaborate canyons and deep ravines. To the south the thin soil becomes slightly more fertile, allowing sparse pine forests to grow. Here the Dark Elves have huge plantations to feed the cities, worked by slaves who labour until they drop dead, their bodies left to decay and nourish the barren soil.

Naggarond, The Tower of Cold

Naggarond is the oldest and largest of the Dark Elves' cities, and quite likely the most evil place in the world. Its black stone walls rise a hundred feet and set within them are four vast gateways with doors of iron fifty feet high. About the ramparts are set a hundred towers, which rise as high above the battlements as the walls above the bare rock of the city's foundations. From these towers fly the dark banners of the Witch King, painted upon the flayed skin of those sacrificed to Khaine. Severed heads and other body parts belonging to those who have displeased Malekith rot upon spikes that spear outwards from the battlements – hundreds of decomposing bodies and crow-savaged skeletons greet those who pass through the gates.

Within the impenetrable walls the city rises higher and higher into the foothills of the mountains and at its centre stands the tower of the Witch King. A mighty fortress in its own right, the citadel of Naggaroth has spawned many smaller towers and a maze of ramparts that jut from its sheer sides. A corona of deadly magic plays about the highest peak of the tower.

It is said that the sorceries of Malekith enable him to look out upon the whole world from the height of his tower, to direct his gaze wherever his malicious intents demand. Under this scornful stare, the armies of the Witch King march to war and his heralds ride all across his lands, taking the will of the Witch King to his furthest domains. From his chambers at the very top of the citadel, the Witch King bends his thoughts and eyes to the mist-shrouded isle of Ulthuan, forever staring at the prize he so desperately wishes to claim.

Naggarond is swathed in a perpetual pall of sacrificial smoke that rises from the burning altars of Khaine, the Lord of Murder. Upon these altars the Death Hags tear men and Elves apart. They pluck beating hearts from living bodies and pull entrails from the bellies of their screaming victims, casting these organs into the sacred flame pits of their bloodthirsty god.

In blood-stained chambers within the walls of the city are the barracks of the Black Guard of Naggarond, the most favoured warriors of the Witch King. Their every whim attended to by an army of slaves, the Black Guard spend their days and nights training for war. In wide drill squares they butcher slaves for weapons practice and offer up the remains to the dark gods of the Elves. Their armouries contain the most ancient and deadly weapons of the Dark Elves – dire swords, halberds and spears that were created in the time of Aenarion or later forged in witchfire and blood by the likes of Hotek and Furion. Other Dark Elves shun the chambers of the Black Guard, for they are quick of temper and will slay any who look upon them and do not show due deference. Thus, their halls are silent except for the screams of the Black Guard's victims and the biting laughter of their captain, Kouran.

Karond Kar, Tower of Despair

The Dark Elves built only one city upon the shores of the Sea of Chill. Most exposed of all the citadels, Karond Kar is swept by gale force winds and deluged with perpetual icy rain. It is to Karond Kar that the majority of slaves are brought from the west, unloaded upon ice-slicked docks, naked to the elements. Not only chains keep them from escaping, for the city stands out on a thin peninsula surrounded by freezing waters. There is no escape from Karond Kar, though thousands have perished attempting to do so, rather than face the cruel attentions of their new owners.

Thousands die as they cross the seas to Karond Kar, stifled and suffocated in the holds of slave ships or tortured to death for the amusement of black-hearted crews. From the docks the slaves are driven amidst jeering crowds, while slave masters beat them forward. Such is their number that those that stumble are doomed to be crushed beneath the feet of their fellows as the whips of the Dark Elves drive them onwards to the markets. At this sight the crowds laugh hard and cry out in pleasure, for such is their love of cruelty this sorry spectacle is considered great entertainment.

The slave markets are vast and those captives that make it to the wide open plazas beyond the docks are roughly examined and divided by age and gender, destined to labour in mines and quarries or serve in the dungeons and kitchens of the great towers. The palaces of the slave traders overlook the markets so that they might see when a ship or Black Ark has returned from its marauding. These palaces are decorated with the bones of slaves that have died on the unforgiving voyages. Using blackest magic, the sorcerers of Karond Kar bind the souls of these unfortunates to their mortal remains, and the city trembles with the wails of these desperate spirits. Even in death the slaves are put to use, for Dark Elves love to hear the shrieks of their dead slaves, a sound of dread and despair. It fills their dreams with delicious images of suffering and pain.

Ghrond, The North Tower

Ghrond lies in the bitterly cold north of the Witch King's domain. In shape it is likened to the great city of Naggarond, yet is far smaller in size, a fortress to be garrisoned rather than a place in which to dwell. Its single, massive tower rises from a mountain spur like a grim, black and slender spear.

From the pinnacle of Ghrond's tower, Sorceresses of the Dark Convent can see far across the tundra, and peer into the ever-shifting Realm of Chaos. Within the Realm of Chaos the lands seethe with energy, rising and falling like the sea, whilst the air is bathed in competing colours of magic, turning and twisting, howling and crying like the wind. The Sorceresses observe the

changes in the Realm of Chaos, for it is said that the patterns of change hold the secrets to the future, and that all mysteries are contained therein for those who dare to look.

Every day dark-clad riders gallop away from the tower of Ghrond bearing the reports of its guardians to Naggarond. These foretell of things to come, of auspicious moments when the Witch King's armies will meet with success, or of the growing power of his enemies. From these observations Malekith plots his strategies and launches his armies upon the world.

Hag Graef, The Dark Crag

Hag Graef is the city most feared by all the Dark Elves' captives, for its name means the Dark Crag and it is well earned. The city has been built at the bottom of a cold, dark valley and is completely surrounded by mountains of bare rock that stretch higher than the highest walls in the world. No sunlight reaches the city of Hag Graef and it is shrouded with perpetual gloom and shadow.

All about the city are the mines and quarries of the Witch King, from which uncountable slaves dig iron and stone to build the fortresses of the Dark Elves. Chained together, the slaves scrape and hack at the rock, often deep underground in narrow tunnels and black passageways. The chill winds bite deep and there is little to eat but scraps of foul dark bread, as Dark Elves like to see their slaves cold and starving, their wills broken, and enjoy beating them all the harder

---

The fishing boat Bonadventure *rose and fell on the immense swell that preceded the coming storm. A black cloud boiled down from the west at surprising speed and the wind grew into a gale ahead of the thunderhead. Fog spread out from under the black cloud, thickening rather than dissipating in the winds, which struck Arnaud Ferond as somewhat unnatural.*

The ship's captain eyed the storm suspiciously as he called to the masthead, but the lookout could see nothing past the thick fog except the flicker of lightning. Within minutes, the heavy bank of cloud had engulfed the fishing vessel, blanketing every direction in gloom. The only sounds were the slapping of waves against the hull, the occasional rumble of thunder and the discontented murmuring of the crew. Trapped in the cloying mists, Arnaud began to grow even more nervous. Something dark and huge reared up in the shadows and at first the captain thought that they had been turned about and were somehow running aground. The cliff towered higher than anything he'd ever seen. He was about to call for the ship to come about, but the words choked in his throat.

The Bonadventure *had broken through a bank of cloud and the full majesty of the Black Ark was revealed; a titanic castle soaring into the storm*

clouds, floating atop a massive granite outcrop. Winged creatures flapped about its minarets and cruel figures in scaled cloaks leered down from savage battlements.

Out of instinct, Arnaud hammered at the warning bell and bellowed out orders. United in their dread, the crew leapt to the sheets to haul the ship onto a new heading, away from the floating citadel. As the fell apparition receded from view, Arnaud let out an explosive sigh of relief.

Their reprieve was short-lived. Water spumed as something burst to the surface ahead of the ship. A gigantic, serpentine beast fully four or five times larger than the Bonadventure *surged out of the water. Atop its back was a slender castle, water foaming from its battlements. Arnaud watched in horror as the monster bore down on him, its many eyes alight with a greenish glow.*

The crew were screaming and shouting and some hurled themselves from the deck in terror. Arnaud's last dread-laden vision was of a jaw filled with dagger-like teeth lunging down and the crash of splintering wood. The interloper dealt with, the Black Ark crashed on through the waves, its course set for L'Anguille

when they collapse from thirst and starvation. Even after death there is no respite, for the mines are riddled with veins and lodes of warpstone – solid magic – that animates the corpses of the dead and keeps them labouring until they decay into piles of bones.

Har Ganeth, City of Executioners

The name of Har Ganeth is cursed with evil. In Ulthuan, none will speak of the city that they call the Cursed Place; whilst to the Dark Elves it is the City of Executioners. Once the High Elves brought battle to Har Ganeth, and attacked the city with as great an army as had ever dared the Witch King's lands. For many days and nights the battle raged without relent, until the High Elves were driven from the field. Many fell as they turned to flee, collapsing from exhaustion. Others were taken captive by swift Dark Riders as they attempted to run. They awoke upon the blood-soaked altars of Khaine. The Witch Elves even took those Dark Elves too weary to offer resistance.

The victory celebration of the Dark Elves was a terrible thing to behold. Captive after captive were brought to the altars and slain in the cruelest ways imaginable. The screams of the dying mingled with the shallow laughter of the Witch Elves as they danced naked about the bodies of the slain. Wine and blood flowed from the altars and drunkenly the Dark Elves praised their evil god. For many nights the sacrificial fires burned, and the Dark Elves feasted upon the flesh of their defeated foes. The Dark Elves were gripped by a madness of death and destruction and fell upon each other in ecstatic violence.

Blood fountained from the windows of the high citadel and ran down the streets like a river. Crimson gore spattered the Temples of Khaine and coloured his brazen idols. The steps of the great Shrine of Khaine were littered with dismembered corpses and spilled entrails. Everywhere laid Elves entwined with each other and covered in blood, stupefied with wine and gorged upon unholy meat, sated upon the horrors of their own depravity. When it was over, the sun rose upon a city stained red with blood, assuring Har Ganeth's infamy in the annals of Ulthuan.

Clar Karond, Tower of Doom

In Clar Karond untold hordes of slaves labour upon the fleets of the Witch King. It is Clar Karond that serves as Malekith's principal shipyards, where the raiding fleets that harry the land of Ulthuan and beyond are built. The city is vast and sprawling, surrounded by forests of towering pines. These black trees are felled for the hulls of the raiding ships by gangs of chained slaves, leaving great swathes of destruction that cut like scars through the woodlands. Nothing but the moans of the slaves' misery and the hewing of wood fills the silent groves, for the Dark Elves have driven all other living things from the dark shadows beneath the boughs of the forest.

West of Clar Karond lies Doom Gate, most easterly of the entrances into the underworld realm. Guarded by seven Hydras, Doom Gate is hidden amongst the

soaring trees of the Black Forests. Dark Elf patrols from Doom Gate scour these woods, seeking escaped slaves and mutant monsters for the fighting pits of Clar Karond. The Corsairs of the city eagerly wager their prizes on these gladiatorial contests, which see humans and Elves pitted against chymeras, bears, Chaos spawn, wolves and each other.

The Underworld Sea

For hundreds of years the raiding fleets of the Dark Elves were confined to the Sea of Chaos and the Great Ocean. Then the Dark Lord of Hag Graef Kaledor Maglen discovered the Underworld Sea, a huge water-filled underground cavern that links the Sea of Chaos to the Broken Land on the eastern coast of the New World. The sea runs under the Black Spine Mountains, and is part of a huge network of caverns and tunnels that honeycomb the great mountain range.

The Underworld Sea, as its name implies, consists of a labyrinthine maze of dark tunnels and strange caves. Movement is dangerous even on the well-known routes, for the threat of cave-ins or flash floods is a constant danger. There are also many strange and extremely predatory creatures that inhabit this unearthly subterranean realm.

The most accomplished explorers of the Underworld Sea come from the tribe of the Shades, mountain-dwellers who forsook the life of the bleak cities in ages past. Yet even they have only uncovered a small fraction of the secrets held by the Underworld Sea. Each decade brings new discoveries, and recently the Shades have been finding increasing evidence that point towards an entire lost civilisation hidden deep within the underground caverns. Who or what these underworld dwellers might be, or how they came to be living so far beneath the world, no one, as yet, can say.

For the moment, the Dark Elves care little about lost races and hidden civilisations. Instead they are glad the Underworld Sea gives them passage to the west, giving them access to the Boiling Sea and beyond, the rich lands of Cathay and Nippon. Now there is no corner of the world safe from the ravages of the Witch King!

The Shadowlands

This benighted realm was once the proud land of Nagarythe, site of Anlec where Aenarion held his court. When Malekith rose to inherit the rule of his father, the people of Nagarythe were grim and warlike, having lived under the terror of the Daemon invasions and the unforgiving rule of Aenarion. Some Naggarothi did not swear fealty to Malekith when he moved for the

Phoenix Throne, and here as elsewhere in Ulthuan the strife of civil war divided houses and set families to fighting amongst themselves. To this day, the descendants of these warring factions battle for possession of their ancestral homelands.

Today what little remains of Nagarythe is known as the Shadowlands. It is a sparse realm, where no cities raise their tall towers above the silent desolation. The Shadow Warriors, loyal to the memory of the ancient Shadow King Alith Anar, stake their claim to these lands, but it is one that the Dark Elves strongly contest. Every year there are battles between the folk of Naggaroth and the Shadow Warriors, every year the curse of Nagarythe claims more victims.

Most prized in the minds of the Dark Elves, and most ill-regarded in the chronicles of the High Elves, is the blasted site of ancient Anlec. Several times this dark castle has been rebuilt and destroyed over successive wars, and the lands about it are so saturated with the blood of Elves that only one plant will grow there – bloodroot, a thorny bramble highly prized by Dark Elf Assassins for its toxic sap. Though it has been scoured by fire and magic, the evil of Anlec still hangs in the air around the blackened rocks, and it is utterly silent, for no birds fly there and no small animals thrive within the twisting bloodroot bushes. Anlec has perhaps claimed more Elven lives, from both sides of the divide, than any other place in Ulthuan.

Along the coast of the Shadowlands rise many small isles, though most of these are little more than strangely formed rocks jutting from the waves. The magic of the Sundering scoured these islands, leaving them as twisted, lifeless places. Residual Dark Magic taints the waters still, and mutant beasts stirred from the lightless depths by the collapse of Nagarythe still lurk in the waters, dragging ships down to a murky demise.

The Boiling Sea

On the west coast of the New World, across the Black Spine Mountains on the opposite side of Naggaroth, lies a region of islands and monster-infested waters known as the Boiling Sea. Only the Black Arks of the Dark Elves dare to enter this inhospitable and dangerous territory, and they do so for one reason only – to capture the monstrous sea creatures that have become such an important part of their fleet.

The Boiling Sea was created many millennia ago, before the recorded history of the Elves had begun. It came about when an immense earthquake rocked the New World. The tumultuous heaving of the lands ripped apart the western coasts and toppled them into the seas.

Vast tracts of cliff tops and shoreline were pulverised and drowned beneath the onrushing sea, creating the patchwork of islands that now run along the length of the coast, which the Elves call the Broken Land.

The earthquake also tore deep rents in the sea bed, terrible chasms like wounds in the world's flesh that have never healed. Through these fissures, molten lava surges up from the world's core, heating the water and creating great bursts of explosive vapours. In parts the sea here literally boils, giving rise to the region's name.

Although many parts of the Boiling Sea are deadly to all forms of life, there are others where the mineral-rich waters teem with all kinds of creatures, ranging from tiny plankton through to leviathan beasts hunted by the Dark Elves. Two of the most infamous monsters used in the Dark Elf fleets are the Sea Dragons and the Helldrakes, both of which are found in considerable numbers around the Boiling Sea. The Sea Dragon is largest of all sea-going monsters; easily capable of carrying a spired castle on its back crewed by Dark Elves. Helldrakes are smaller but even more ferocious, combining the ferocity of a wolverine with claws and fangs capable of shredding the ships of the Dark Elves' prey.

With more and more of these creatures brought back from the Boiling Sea, the Dark Elf fleets have changed dramatically. Traditional warships are widely scorned, and now many Black Arks are accompanied solely by flotillas of these terrors of the ocean waves.

The Blighted Isle

At the very northern tip of Ulthuan lies the Shadowlands, all that remains of the land that was shattered and destroyed when the Witch King attempted to unbound the spells that contained the Realm of Chaos. Rising from the misty seas is the Blighted Isle, largest of the islands, home to the forbidding Shrine of Khaine. The Elves have long since abandoned this dark and rocky isle, but it is still a place of great power and deep significance.

The shrine itself is a massive black altar in which is embedded the Sword of Khaine, the ultimate weapon. The sword is as old as the world; a shard of the fatal weapon forged by the Elven smith god Vaul for Khaine; a fragment of crystallised death capable of slaying mortals, Daemons and gods. The only mortal being to wield the Sword of Khaine was Aenarion, and in doing so fulfilled a prophecy that cursed the Elves to aeon of tragedy and his line to eternal damnation.

The shrine sits on a vast plain covered with bones and skulls. Many battles have been fought between the Dark Elves and the High Elves for control of the shrine, and at night the spirits of slain warriors drift over the battlefield locked in eternal conflict, forever captured by the will of Khaine. The struggle for the Shrine of Khaine is symbolic of the struggle in the soul of the Elf race, between those who follow darkness and those who seek some measure of harmony. None can say how this struggle will end, or indeed, if it ever will.

DARK ELF BESTIARY

In this section you will find information and rules for all of the different warriors, heroes, monsters and war machines used in the Dark Elves army. At the end of the section are some special characters – infamous Dark Elves that you can field in your army.

Dark Elves are bitter, vicious killers that detest all other creatures – even other Dark Elves! Druchii warriors love nothing more than to see their enemies screaming in pain, and take pleasure from spilling blood and spreading misery. They are relentlessly aggressive in battle, shouting praises to their black gods as they cut down their foes.

The Dark Elves reserve their deepest enmity for the High Elves of Ulthuan, who they see as treacherous usurpers. For over five thousand years, the armies of Naggaroth have waged war upon their kin. Battles between Dark Elves and High Elves are exceptionally bloody, as the Dark Elves hurl themselves at their foes with unending ferocity and the warriors of Ulthuan stoically stand their ground despite the terrifying beasts and merciless agonies unleashed upon them.

On the following pages are the complete rules for the models in the Dark Elf army. Each entry includes the model's profile and special rules. This is normally used in combination with the army list on pages 89-103 to create a force that can be used in a one-off game of Warhammer. However, players can also design scenarios with specific forces involved, or run a series of games in a campaign, both of which may well use the information in this section without recourse to the Dark Elves army list.

Khainites

Some Dark Elves are utterly dedicated to Khaine, the Elven god of murder. They are merciless killers who have no qualms about shedding Dark Elf blood as much as any other kind. Consequently, they are the least-trusted warriors in all of Dark Elf society. These units are noted in the Bestiary as being Khainite.

Only Khainite characters may join a Khainite unit. In addition, certain special rules and magic items affect Khainite units differently – the Cauldron of Blood, for example. Note that Khainite characters may still join non-Khainite units. This means that you could use a Death Hag as a leader for a unit of Dark Elf Warriors, for example.

Special Rules

Many troop types have special rules to reflect their unique nature and abilities, and these are explained in the individual Bestiary entries that follow. To save space and repetition, where a model has a special rule that is explained in the Warhammer rulebook, only the name of the rule is given in this section. Refer to the Special Rules section of Warhammer for the full details of how the rule works. Similarly, the following rule applies to the majority of the units in this Bestiary, and as such is detailed here:

Eternal Hatred: All models with this rule Hate all opposing models (Hatred is explained in the Warhammer rulebook). In addition, such is their detestation of their cousins from Ulthuan that when fighting against a High Elves army, Dark Elves may re-roll missed close combat attacks in every round of combat, not just the first. Remember that Hatred also applies to mounts as long as their riders are alive.

DARK ELF WARRIORS

The Dark Elves are descendants of the brave warriorfolk that dwelt in Nagarythe during the reign of Aenarion. They are raised from birth as soldiers and raiders, learning early on in their lives that they have only that which they can take. Though their natural mistrust and selfishness occasionally undermines discipline, Dark Elves make up for this with heartfelt bitterness and are united by their mutual loathing for all other creatures.

Regiments of Dark Elves are made up of warriors, both male and female, drawn from the same city, and often the same extended family. Such formations are usually agreed upon not long before battle, as shifting politics and sudden promotions or executions make any kind of formal army structure impossible. Dark Elves sworn to a particular lord or ruling house will fight under the banner of their masters, though this has been known to change over time, and some regiments may even shift loyalty within the course of a battle! The commanders of the army instill a semblance of control by appointing leadership of the regiments to lesser family members, usually younger siblings or bastard offspring with very little standing in the circles of power.

The principle weapon of a Dark Elf soldier is the heavy-bladed spear known in the Druchii tongue as the

Drannach – the Sky-Piercer. The role of these warriors is to defend against enemy counter-attacks threatening the flanks of other formations, and to protect the army's war machines and missile troops. All Elves are swift, and Druchii spear regiments can march quickly to seize ground or respond to the enemy general's plan. These spear troops provide a solid cadre of soldiers that allows the more unstable warriors in the army to roam freely, slaughtering at will.

A proportion of a city's warriors train in the use of the lethal repeater crossbow known as the Uraithen – literally translated as the Deathrain. Regiments armed with this weapon can stand back and unleash a storm of iron tipped bolts against approaching foes, or move forward and cut down enemy ranks to weaken the foe's line before the Dark Elf attack charges in. In particular, the repeater crossbow is favoured by warriors sent to garrison the northern watchtowers, as it is deadly against the lightly armoured tribesmen that foray south in large numbers from the Chaos Wastes.

Dark Elf armies are normally raised by the lords of Naggaroth, in some cases by the Witch King himself and rarely without his leave; nobles that gather large bodies of troops without Malekith's permission tend to incur his fatal suspicion. Such forces are usually gathered for a specific attack, or to bolster the crew for a particular raiding voyage. Dark Elf fleets are continuously sailing across the world to loot the settlements of other races, stealing the treasure they can find and imprisoning the inhabitants to be taken back to Naggaroth. The Witch King also requires huge numbers of Druchii soldiers for the ongoing war with the High Elves of Ulthuan. When fighting these most hated of foes, the Dark Elves are intent only upon wholesale destruction.

	M	WS	BS	S	T	W	I	A	LD
Dark Elf Warrior	5	4	4	3	3	1	5	1	8
Lordling	5	4	4	3	3	1	5	2	8
Guardmaster	5	4	5	3	3	1	5	1	8

Special Rules
Eternal Hatred.

Repeater Crossbow

Used almost exclusively by the warriors of Naggaroth, the repeater crossbow unleashes a hail of deadly darts. Using a sophisticated magazine and loading mechanism it is able to fire a volley of bolts in the same time it takes an ordinary crossbowman to fire a single shot.

Maximum range: 24"; **Strength:** 3

Rules: 2 x multiple shots, armour piercing

BLACK ARK CORSAIRS

When Malekith attempted to destroy the vortex of
Ulthuan, the magical explosion caused most of
Nagarythe to topple into the seas. To save what they
could from the devastation, Malekith and his wizards
cast enchantments upon their citadels so that they rose
up above the crashing waves. Some of these became
the foundations of the cities of the Dark Elves; many
still wander the oceans and seas, manned by reavers
seeking fresh slaughter and loot.

These Black Arks are home to thousands of Corsairs,
hardened fighters who have spent their whole lives
plundering the lands of others. These Corsairs also
form the crews of other vessels, fighting from towers
built upon the backs of the Sea Dragons and Helldrakes
that have become popular in the ports of Naggaroth.

The Corsairs are lauded amongst Dark Elf society for
their daring and bravery. The crews of the Black Arks
embody the drive for a Dark Elf to earn riches and
glory, no matter the cost. For years at a time the
Corsairs ply their bloody trade across the seas, seeking
to return to the adulation of their peers, with enough
slaves and wealth to set themselves up as princes. It is
a hard, dangerous life in the raiding fleets, but a
successful voyage of a decade – a comparatively short
time in the centuries-long life of an Elf – can see the
captain and his crew return with enough wealth and
influence to buy a position in Malekith's court or to
marry into one of the powerful dynasties that rule the
six cities of Naggaroth.

Black Ark Corsairs often fight on the decks of ships or
through the twisting streets of a coastal town, leaping
from mast to mast or roof to roof in stunning displays
of fearless acrobatics. For this reason, Corsairs arm
themselves with a wide variety of vicious cutlasses
and serrated blades, which they can use equally well
in either hand or two at a time. Some Corsairs prefer
to use a handbow; a compact, one-handed version of
the repeater crossbow, which lacks the range of the
larger weapon but is equally lethal at close quarters.
Corsairs also equip themselves with barbed nets,
whips, grapples and such, to allow them to catch
escaping victims and drag them screaming back to be
sliced apart or borne away.

	M	WS	BS	S	T	W	I	A	LD
Corsair	5	4	4	3	3	1	5	1	8
Reaver	5	4	4	3	3	1	5	2	8

Special Rules
Eternal Hatred.

Slavers: When a unit breaks from combat against
Corsairs, the fleeing unit may be ensnared. The Dark
Elf player may force his opponent to re-roll the highest
D6 rolled for the unit's flee distance, before making the
Corsairs' pursuit roll.

Sea Dragon Cloak
Made from the scales of creatures from the Boiling
Sea, these cloaks can be drawn close around the
body to protect against arrows and bullets.

A Sea Dragon cloak adds +1 to a model's saving
throw in close combat, and +2 against any other
attacks (including spells, shooting, and so on). It
may be combined with other armour as normal.

Repeater Handbow
Repeater handbows do not suffer the usual to hit
penalties for shooting at long range or for moving
and shooting.

Repeater handbows require very little time to fire
and so can always be used to stand & shoot against
a charging enemy, even if the enemy starts its charge
within half of its charge distance.

Maximum range: 8"; **Strength:** 3

Rules: 2 x multiple shots (4 x multiple shots if
used as a pair).

BLACK GUARD OF NAGGAROND

Dark Elves are selfish and power-hungry, ever seeking to claw their way to power over the corpses of their kin. As ruler of such an iniquitous people, Malekith trusts none of his fellow Druchii, except occasionally his mother, Morathi. Though no Dark Elf could be described as truly loyal, the Black Guard are the Witch King's favoured warriors, given the sacred task of acting as his personal enforcers and bodyguards. To be allowed so close to the Witch King, these Dark Elves must prove their loyalty to him. Those that endure and survive the strict regime of the Black Guard earn themselves great privilege in the court of Naggarond.

The Black Guard are recruited from the offspring of families in favour with the Witch King, taken at birth from their mothers. With no family ties to distract them, these children are raised within the barracks of the Black Guard and taught the warrior skills required to be Malekith's elite. As soon as they are able, these young novitiates are pitched against each other in fights to the death, so that only the strongest, quickest-witted and most merciless killers survive. Over the years as they mature, these fledgling fighters are regularly visited by the Witch King, who rewards those who show great cunning and bloodthirst. This violence is not restricted to the training fields, and in the early years, a particular intake of recruits can lose up to half their number to murders and fights.

When the aspirants come of age, they are brought before the Witch King and kneel at his feet to swear their undying devotion. It is then that Malekith promises each of them great wealth and lands, which is to be theirs if they serve him well for two hundred years. Those Black Guard that survive this arduous tour of duty go on to become rulers of cities, leaders of armies and favoured members of Malekith's court.

The barracks of the Black Guard are divided into twenty 'Towers', which compete against each other in contests of war and torture. Rivalry between the Towers is encouraged by the Witch King, and each year a bloody tournament is held to determine which Tower will hold dominance over the others. The leaders of these factions are the Tower Masters, veterans of the Black Guard so inculcated with death and battle that they choose to continue in Malekith's service after their two centuries of duty have expired.

	M	WS	BS	S	T	W	I	A	LD
Black Guard	5	5	4	3	3	1	6	2	9
Tower Master	5	5	4	3	3	1	6	3	9

Special Rules
Eternal Hatred, Immune to Psychology, Stubborn.

Warrior Elite: Black Guard may re-roll any failed roll to hit in combat.

ERETH KHIAL

The supreme goddess of the Underworld is Ereth Khial and she is second in power only to Asuryan. In the days before the rise of the Everqueen, Ereth Khial attempted to seduce Asuryan and when he resisted her, she flew into a rage and stole the souls of the Elves and imprisoned them in a black pit, known as Mirai. It is said if ever Ereth Khial is so angered again, she will raise the dead, who will outnumber the living and eat them!

Ereth Khial's most feared servants are the Rephallim – invisible wraith-creatures who lead souls to the underworld and keep them imprisoned there. Worshippers of Ereth Khial hide themselves amongst Ulthuan society. They perform vile ceremonies entreating their goddess to send the wicked Rephallim to snatch away important High Elf counsellors, military leaders and mages. They summon the avatars of Ereth Khial with dark rites and set them upon their foes using talismans unique to each victim – effigies made using the target's hair or blood, or treasured items stolen from the prey's home.

HAR GANETH EXECUTIONERS

Har Ganeth is the spiritual centre of Khaine's worship, with many shrines to the Lord of Murder, dominated by the towering edifice of the great temple. It is from Har Ganeth that Hellebron rules over the Witch Elves, and countless victims are brought here to be sacrificed upon Khaine's altars. It was in Har Ganeth that the first ceremonies of execution were held. Following a great victory over a High Elf army that had foolishly attacked the city, thousands of Elves were taken to the pinnacle of the temple and beheaded by the guards. Such was the delight of the Dark Elves when they saw the heads tumbling down the steps that the executions have become a regular feature of Har Ganeth society.

The guards are so adept that they are now known as the Executioners of Har Ganeth. Each Executioner spends half his waking day in his duties as sentry, and the other half practising with his blade. It is said that a fully-trained Executioner knows the way to kill any creature with a single blow, whether by decapitation, disembowelment or a single thrust through the heart. The Executioners are not frenetic butchers, but rather are cold-blooded killers who take pride in dispatching their foes with the minimum of effort. They are heartless murderers, who see their role as a sacred one, and unlike other Dark Elves do not make sport of their victims, but kill them swiftly and cleanly.

The chosen weapon of one of Khaine's anointed Executioners is the draich. Each draich is forged by the Executioner who wields it, under the supervision of the armourers of the great temple. As an Executioner learns his bloody skills, he also crafts his weapon so that the two are as one. Some Executioners prefer a heavy axe-like blade, others a slender sword, depending upon their own abilities and preferred method of killing.

	M	WS	BS	S	T	W	I	A	LD
Executioner	5	5	4	4	3	1	5	1	8
Draich-master	5	5	4	4	3	1	5	2	8

Special Rules
Eternal Hatred, Killing Blow, Khainite.

Draich
The ritual weapon of one of Khaine's anointed Executioners, each draich is hand-crafted by the armourers of Khaine's temples and may take the form of a vicious sword or a mighty axe. In fact, the word 'draich' represents the act of execution itself, and the skill of the bearer as much as the specific blade used for the ritual.

KHELTHRAI

The word Khelthrai means Bloody Death, and it is the only name by which this deadly warrior is known. Though Anethra Helbane has had slain all but a few of the Elves who know of his true origins, Khelthrai's history is one of secret pride to the Helbane family. Youthful and ambitious, seeking more powerful allies than his own family could provide, Khelthrai killed his own mother to prove his loyalty to the Helbanes. His ruthlessness and dedication were quickly recognised and in return Anethra had her granddaughter Ylandria induct the young Dark Elf into the cult of Executioners in Har Ganeth. Now a highly skilled killer, the threat of Khelthrai's lethal attentions has quelled opposition to the Helbanes for many centuries, and his blade stands ever ready to dispatch those who would move against his adopted family.

SHADES

The Shades are a group of Dark Elves who eschew life in the cities of Naggaroth and instead lead a savage existence in the grim Blackspine Mountains. They are scouts without compare, able to move as swiftly and silently as ghosts through thick forest, across razor-sharp rocks and along the twisting caverns of the Underworld Sea. Companies of Shades disembark from the fleet under cover of darkness, before moving inland to locate targets for the Dark Elves' raids. From hidden positions, they spy on the opposing forces, determining their location and strength, and ambush enemy pickets and outriders to conceal the presence of the Dark Elf army.

When the warriors of the fleet attack, the Shades use their skills to infiltrate behind the enemy battle line, from which position they can harass the foe as they advance, or strike out and slay the crew of war machines. Hardened to the harsh climate of the Blackspine Mountains and locked in an eternal battle with the ferocious creatures of Naggaroth, the Shades are well-armed and canny fighters. All carry repeater crossbows that they use for hunting, while many carry extra swords and daggers, or heavier blades.

The Shades were once city-dwellers like other dark Elves and formed the ruling elite of Clar Karond. It was nobles and warriors from the Shade family that were keenest to explore the Underworld Sea, seeking a passage to the western coast. As their explorations took them further and further into the dark, unknown chambers, their enemies in Clar Karond gathered against them. Eventually they were ousted from power, and rather than serve as slaves to their usurpers, they chose voluntary exile in the harsh mountains. For a score of centuries the Shades have lived in the mountains, learning the secrets of survival in one of the fiercest climes in the world. The rulers of Clar Karond fear that one day the Shades will return to stake their claim to the city, but this is unlikely, for the clans of the Shades now seem more at home on wind-swept mountain ridges and in shadowy canyons.

Even amongst the vicious Dark Elves, the Shades are considered feral, for they practice all manner of strange, unforgiving rites. Their children are abandoned outside the camps on midwinter's eve and are expected to survive and find their way home. Animal sacrifices made to the beating of drums liven the cold nights whilst the Shades drink fermented blood, and the tents of the Shades are made from the skins of their prey – whether Elf, Man, Orc or other beast.

THE SUNKEN ISLES

The war over possession of the ancient realm of Nagarythe, now a shattered series of isles, waxes as strong now as it did five thousand years ago.

In an attempt to wrest control of these lands from the Shadow Warriors of Ulthuan – descendants of Nagarythe renegades who would not swear fealty to Malekith – the Witch King has moved several Shade clans to the Shadowlands to fight against the interlopers defiling the ground of Nagarythe.

Malekith has promised these Shades clans possession of any Nagarythe lands that they can wrest from the High Elves, and rewards them for every head of a Shadow Warrior sent to him in Naggarond. There is now sporadic but vicious guerrilla fighting between the Shadow Warriors of Ulthuan and these emigre Shades – sometimes called the Sundered Clans or Reaver Shades. Malekith hopes that this fighting will sap the strength and morale of the Shadow Warriors, so that they will be swept away when the time for full invasion comes again.

	M	WS	BS	S	T	W	I	A	LD
Shade	5	5	5	3	3	1	5	1	8
Bloodshade	5	5	6	3	3	1	5	2	8

Special Rules
Eternal Hatred, Skirmishers, Scouts.

DARK RIDERS

In the grim days when armies of Daemons besieged Ulthuan, the daemonic hordes could attack at any place, at any time. Able to appear from the Realm of Chaos at will, the armies of the Chaos Gods could strike without warning. Aenarion's hosts stood ready to repel any attack, and across Nagarythe and the other realms keen-eyed watchers kept guard for any daemonic intrusion.

These scouts rode upon black steeds from Nagarythe – fast and hardy mounts that could gallop for a day without tiring. The riders wore cloaks of raven feathers, enchanted with spells of shadow to keep them hidden from the eyes of the enemy, and so were known as the Raven Heralds. When armies of the Daemons appeared from the Realm of Chaos, these scouts would ride to warn the Phoenix King, so that the army of the Elves could march forth and battle the Daemons. The sight of one of these heralds galloping across the hills and along mountain passes became a familiar sight in those troubled times and they were hailed as heroic guardians of Ulthuan.

During the civil war, these riders earned a more sinister reputation. They rode ahead of the hosts of Nagarythe, spying out the positions of the Phoenix King's armies and locating sites for ambush or attack.

Not only this, but the Naggarothi Dark Riders would also sow terror and confusion amongst the populace of the other kingdoms, burning villages and towns and driving their people into the wilds where they could be hunted down. The Dark Riders gloried in the thrill of the chase, and thought nothing of running down innocent victims. The Dark Riders have continued in this vein to the present day, as well as fulfiling the role of swift messengers between the ruling families of Naggaroth's six cities.

In battle, the Dark Riders swiftly outflank the enemy to attack war machines and cut lines of supply, skewering their victims upon their barbed spears. Many Dark Riders carry repeater crossbows so that they can hunt their prey from afar, cutting down enemy light cavalry and skirmishers with a hail of black-fletched bolts.

	M	WS	BS	S	T	W	I	A	LD
Dark Rider	5	4	4	3	3	1	5	1	8
Herald	5	4	5	3	3	1	5	2	8
Dark Steed	9	3	0	3	3	1	4	1	5

Special Rules
Eternal Hatred, Fast Cavalry.

ELLINILL

Ellinill is a many-faced god of destruction. He has more than a hundred guises, with which he wreaks mayhem and havoc upon the world. Each has a separate name and appearance, such as Hukon the god of earthquakes, Addaioth the god of volcanoes and Estreuth the god of drought.

In the times before the Sundering, offerings of flowers, floating lamps and burned incense were used to appease him. In this way, the High Elves of Lothern still pay peaceful homage to Ellinill in his guise of Mathlann, god of storms.

However, the Dark Elves' worship of Ellinill is not so peaceful. From towering cliffs and upon the decks of their ships, the Druchii sacrifice living creatures to bring safe passage for their Black Arks or to unleash a tempest upon their enemies. Often Corsairs will chain some of their captured slaves to the prows of their ships in appeasement of Ellinill.

Some shrines to Ellinill are built over deep, lava-filled chasms in the mountains of Naggaroth. These pillared temples resonate with the chanting of priests and the screams of captives as they are hurled into the fiery depths in exchange for favours from the Lord of Destruction.

WITCH ELVES

enough not to succumb to their wounds are rounded up by the Witch Elves after the battle is over. These poor souls are torn apart in victory celebrations, their blood used as grateful libations to the Lord of Murder.

The Hags and Death Hags that lead the Witch Elves are privy to the innermost secrets of the cult. It is they who mix the noxious potions that drive the Witch Elves into their battle-rage. They carry ancient weapons from the vaults of the temples and know the secret names of their god that can befuddle their foes or strike them down. The war-skills of these priestesses have been honed over centuries of fighting, and their battle-lust knows no limits. The highest-ranking priestesses are the Hag Queens, who bathe in the Cauldrons of Blood to rejuvenate their bodies. The oldest of the Hag Queens have ruled over the cult for thousands of years.

	M	WS	BS	S	T	W	I	A	LD
Witch Elf	5	4	4	3	3	1	6	1	8
Hag	5	4	4	3	3	1	6	2	8
Death Hag	5	6	6	4	3	2	8	3	9

Special Rules
Eternal Hatred, Frenzy, Khainite, Poisoned Attacks.

The Dark Elves worship many dark and forbidden gods, but by far the most prominent is Khaine, the Lord of Murder. His is the largest cult in Dark Elf society, ruled over by priestesses known as Hag Queens, the mistresses of the Brides of Khaine – the Witch Elves. Khaine demands bloody, agonising sacrifice, for he is a god of death and suffering. Every Dark Elf city has at least one temple dedicated to Khaine, and there is a shrine to the Lord of Murder within every Black Ark. By far the largest temple is found in Har Ganeth where, day and night, constant sacrifices are made to the Bloody-handed God.

The Witch Elves drive themselves into an ecstatic fervour during their brutal ceremonies as they rip hearts from chests and fling them into iron braziers, daub runes of Khaine onto their bodies with their victims' blood and decorate the altars of their bloodthirsty master with bones and entrails. They are no less vicious in battle. They are the most cruel of all the Dark Elves, and the most bloodthirsty. Before battle, Witch Elves drink blood laced with poisonous herbs, which drives them into a frenzy of bloodlust. They do not carry shields, caring nothing for their own protection, and are armed with sharp swords and long knives whose edges are dipped in venom. Once battle begins, the Witch Elves hurl themselves at their foes, ripping apart their enemies with a storm of poisoned blades. Those foes unfortunate

THE BRIDES OF BURNING BLOOD

The Brides of Burning Blood are one of a growing number of Witch Elf cults that have no permanent shrine in any of the Dark Elf cities. They prefer to worship Khaine solely on the battlefield, where the gore soaked ground is their altar, and the blood of their foes their offering to the bloody-handed god. They have little interest in taking live captives back to Naggaroth, for they believe that blood spilt in the heat of battle, where it is raw and still filled with both fear and anger, is amongst the most treasured by Khaine. As Khaine is also the lord of suffering, the Brides make use of a rare poison with which they coat their wicked blades, a toxin that literally boils the blood of its victims. Any that are cut by such a blade die in fits of agonised screams, their own steaming lifeblood erupting from ruptured arteries.

After a battle the gore-soaked Brides are brought before the Death Hag one at a time. Should more than a few patches of skin be discovered that have not been touched by an offering to Khaine – namely blood spilt in battle – then it will be decreed that the sacrifices made were unacceptable to the Lord of Murder. In a frenzy of repentant fury, the Witch Elves then seek out other victims and will fall upon them with renewed vigour. It matters not if these victims are other Dark Elves, so eager are the Brides to spill blood in the name of their merciless god.

CAULDRON OF BLOOD

The Cauldrons of Blood are rumoured to be gifts from Khaine, who bestowed them upon the Witch Elves as reward for their single-minded dedication to his cause. Or so claimed Morathi when she gave the first of the Cauldrons to the Cult of Khaine. Each Cauldron takes the form of a huge pot made of solid brass, covered with arcane runes that flicker and glow with a magical light. The Cauldron is kept filled with the blood of countless victims sacrificed by the Witch Elves. Curiously it never over-fills, and always maintains the same level no matter how many gallons of the unfortunate victim's life-blood are poured into it. Each Cauldron is tended by a Death Hag called the Keeper of the Cauldron. The Cauldrons are normally kept safely within the Witch Elf city temples, but are brought forth and travel with the Witch Elf contingent as they march to battle. The presence of a Cauldron of Blood inspires the Dark Elves to an even greater pitch of war-lust, while its magical properties serve to sustain them.

	M	WS	BS	S	T	W	I	A	LD
Hag	5	4	4	3	3	1	6	2	8

Special Rules
Eternal Hatred, Frenzy, Khainite, War Machine, Terror, Magic Resistance (1), Poisoned Attacks.

Attendants: The Death Hag and the two Hags are treated as a war machine crew, though they are deployed at the same time as characters. The Cauldron gives its attendants a 4+ ward save. The attendants never pursue, even though they have the Hatred rule. The Cauldron cannot be damaged – ignore any hits allocated against it. If its attendants are killed it is removed immediately.

Blessings of Khaine: The attendants, even if engaged in combat, may use one of the blessings below in their Start of Turn phase, after all Psychology tests are taken.

Pick a single friendly unit within 24" of the Cauldron, even if engaged in close combat, to be affected by the chosen blessing. The chosen effect lasts until the start of the unit's next turn. This is not a spell and cannot be be dispelled or otherwise stopped. A unit may only be affected by a single blessing per turn, even if you have more than one Cauldron of Blood.

Fury of Khaine: All models in the unit gain +1 Attack.

Strength of Khaine: All models in the unit gain killing blow in close combat.

Bloodshield of Khaine: All models in the unit gain a 5+ ward save.

Note that mounts and creatures pulling a chariot are not affected by the blessings.

Altar of Khaine: All Khainite units within 12" of a Cauldron of Blood become Stubborn.

DEATH NIGHT

Witch Elves live in the temples of Khaine under the glowering eyes of their Hag Queens. The Hag Queens are extremely ancient, and once a year they take part in the riotous celebrations of Death Night. The streets echo with manic drumming and the shrill pipes of the temples, while blood-red incense drifts across squares and down alleys in thick clouds that swathe Khaine's beloved hunters. Groups of depraved Witch Elves prowl the streets and steal away any Dark Elves they find, sometimes breaking into houses to take petrified inhabitants away for sacrifice.

On Death Night the Hag Queens bathe in blood to restore themselves, at which time they are the most enchanting and voluptuous of all Elves, their strangely cadaverous beauty more powerful and captivating than any magic. Over the year they revert into the haggard crones that they really are, until Death Night comes round once more and Dark Elves hide in their homes, listening to the revelry and evil laughter of the midnight celebrations of the Witch Elves.

COLD ONE KNIGHTS

Considered by many to be the most fearsome of all the Dark Elves' dreaded warriors, the Cold One Knights form a devastating shock elite. The skill of the knights and the viciousness of their mounts sets them above the cavalry of lesser races. They are often found at the forefront of the attack, smashing into the enemies' most deadly regiments.

It is a daring Dark Elf who purchases a Cold One to ride, for the lizards savagely attack all who come near them, recognising warm-blooded creatures by their smell. This is dangerous in itself and no few strutting nobles have been savaged by their own mounts, much to the amusement of their rivals. To avoid this, the Dark Elf must anoint himself repeatedly with the foul-smelling slime of the Cold Ones so that the beasts will accept him.

There is a great price to pay for the Dark Elf, though, for the fumes of this noxious balm are extremely potent, burning the nostrils, numbing the skin and destroying taste buds, so that the rider can no longer smell or taste food, or feel the touch of a lover. So it is that a Cold One is both a fearsome war-mount, and also a declaration of bravery and ambition on the part of the knight. For many Dark Elves, this heavy price is considered one worth paying, for in doing so a warrior

proves his dedication to the Witch King and can earn great political as well as physical reward. A fully armed and armoured Cold One Knight carries a long lance known as a kheitai, or 'soul eater'. His mount is protected by layers of scaled skin and tears apart its victims with curved claws and dagger-long fangs. Cold Ones are dim-witted in the extreme, however, and even when broken for a rider are notoriously truculent. To master such a beast requires not only skill, but also physical strength and immense willpower. Though they are few in number, the ferocity of the Cold One Knights is such a decisive weapon that they can win a hard-fought battle with a single devastating charge.

	M	WS	BS	S	T	W	I	A	LD
Cold One Knight	5	5	4	4	3	1	6	1	9
Dread Knight	5	5	4	4	3	1	6	2	9
Cold One	7	3	0	4	4	1	2	1	3

Special Rules
Eternal Hatred, Fear, Stupidity.

Thick-skinned: Due to their thick hides, Cold Ones give a +2 bonus to their rider's saving throw instead of the normal +1 save given to cavalry models.

NETHU

Nethu is Ereth Khial's son and he is the doorkeeper of Mirai, the Underworld. He carries a silver harp that he uses to tease the soul of an Elf from his body and a heavy iron key for the gates of Mirai. Rites of Nethu allow converse with the spirits of the dead and there are legends of daring Elves who have tricked Nethu to gain access to the Underworld and learnt the secrets of the deceased. Some Dark Elves wear amulets of Nethu fashioned from bone bound with raw sinew to protect against disease.

Agents of Malekith living within the cities of Ulthuan carve secret runes of Nethu upon the chambers of High Elf nobles and civic dignitaries. Once ensorcelled, their victims suffer a wasting ennui that drains both body and spirit. Those cursed in this way are driven mad by the potent hex. Some believe it was the power of Nethu that allowed Malekith to twist and torment the dreams of Morvael. After Ashantir Lightweaver cast himself from the pinnacle of the Tower of Hoeth, such a rune was found by the Swordmasters under the dead mage's bed. This led to a desperate hunt for the cultists that had placed it there. The search caused untold shock and grief that lasted for nearly a year, after which the Loremasters decreed that the agents had long since fled and escaped retribution.

COLD ONE CHARIOT

Amongst the Dark Elves it is a symbol of great prestige and favour to ride into battle upon the magnificent chariots of Naggarond. These are given as gifts to warriors who have pleased the lord Malekith with their devotion, bravery and prowess in battle. Accompanied by the roars of the Cold Ones and the thunder of wheels across the battlefield, a chariot smashing into the enemy is a sight magnificent to behold for the Dark Elves. The Cold Ones tear apart those that survive the barbed tips of the crew's long spears and the chariot's scythed wheels.

On occasion the Witch King himself rides to battle upon the legendary Black Chariot and, such is the fickle nature of Dark Elf loyalty, this is often followed by a clamour from other nobles to show their support and possess such a war machine for themselves. Of course, the armour-clad Witch King can no longer feel or smell as a mortal, so is immune to the stench of the Cold Ones – something that comes as a great shock for a noble seeking to make a mark for himself by emulating his ruler in this fashion.

	M	WS	BS	S	T	W	I	A	LD
Chariot	-	-	-	5	5	4	-	-	-
Charioteer	-	5	4	4	-	-	6	1	9
Cold One	7	3	0	4	-	-	2	1	-

Special Rules
**Eternal Hatred, Fear, Stupidity,
3+ Armour saving throw.**

Since their discovery, Cold Ones, known in the Druchii tongue as Nauglir, have become ever more popular as mounts for the so-called nobles of Naggaroth. The natural viciousness of these fearsome beasts resonates with the Dark Elf love of violence. Both rider and mount share a mutual lack of mercy for their prey, which has resulted in many bloody and ferocious slaughters upon the battlefield.

The first Cold Ones were ridden by Amarekh Khail and his companions, who shattered the High Elves' line at Athel Oreirian. These riders became infamous amongst the High Elves for decades, and were easily recognisable by the banner they flew – a macabre standard made from the bones and skins of those slain in their first battle.

The Cold One chariot regiment known as the Bloodscythes were equally lauded amongst the Naggarothi some three thousand years later. With their distinctive red-lacquered weapons and armour they became a familiar sight amongst the hosts of Hag Graef and were instrumental in many victories until their leader, Asdrual Severain, fell to an Assassin's blade. The remnants of the regiment slew each other in

the ensuing power struggle, before the survivors finally disbanded and went their separate ways.

Such infighting is commonplace amongst the arrogant princes who ride these beasts. Two brothers, Venien and Hurien, became renowned generals and jointly led the hosts of House Heghlin in several decisive triumphs during the most recent campaigns in Nagarythe. Despite their success, ultimately they were unable to share the glory. Hurien took the cloak of his brother and soaked it in the blood of a mountain boar. When Venien came to attend his mount, the scent, which Venien could not smell due to the sense-numbing elixir he had applied, the Cold One went wild and tore the Dark Elf lord to pieces. Hurien ruled House Heghlin for another fifteen hundred years, never admitting that his brother's death was anything more than an unfortunate accident.

The oldest Cold One, as far as the Dark Elves know, was named Kintearer and lived for seventeen hundred and thirty two years after it was captured. During this time it served as the mount of three different generals, including Anglan Arheirain, the infamous slayer of Loremaster Menthrith of the White Tower.

REAPER BOLT THROWER

Reapers are used at sea to clear the decks of enemy vessels, and on land to scythe down entire ranks of enemy warriors. A mechanism of counterweights and cords allows the Reaper to shoot a hail of bolts, or a single missile with greater force. The bolts of the Reaper are barbed and difficult to remove from wounds without causing greater injury and torment. Casualties that suffer such horrendous injuries that they are worthless as slaves are left by the Dark Elves to bleed to death or given over to the bloody caresses of the Witch Elves.

Firing the Reaper

Repeater Bolt Throwers can fire in one of two ways. In each Shooting phase, the Repeater Bolt Thrower may either shoot a single bolt (see the rule book under Bolt Throwers) or may fire a volley. If using the volley option then the Repeater Bolt Thrower shoots six bolts in the Shooting phase. These shots cannot pierce ranks and only inflict one wound each, rather than D3. All bolts must be directed against a single target. Volleys have a range of 48", Strength 4, with armour saves suffering a -2 penalty. The Repeater Bolt Thrower is incredibly accurate and is not subject to the multiple shots special weapon rule.

	M	WS	BS	S	T	W	I	A	LD
Dark Elf	5	4	4	3	3	1	5	1	8
Reaper	-	-	-	-	7	3	-	-	-

Special Rules

Eternal Hatred, War Machine.

The tolling of an alarm bell rang out over the rooftops of the squalid coastal town. As Alandriakh watched from amongst the trees upon a nearby hilltop, smoke and flames wreathed the human hovels. He fondly imagined the terrified shouts, the wild eyes of the clumsy humans as they dashed about in panic; their cries of torment as Meurlith's Corsairs cut them down or bound them in barbed nets.

With a wistful sigh, the Dark Elf returned to the Reaper bolt throwers stationed in the copse of trees overlooking the road from the east. Following its course inland, Alandriakh could just about see the squat towers of the castle supposedly protecting this stretch of the shore. He knew that what they did was important, but still it chafed his pride to be so far from the true fighting.

"Let us offer prayers to Khaine that we shall see some blood today," Alandriakh said and in reply received cruel smiles from the crews of the other two Reapers. It was not long before Alandriakh's keen ears picked up the jingling of harnesses and the thud of hooves on the muddy road. He hissed a warning to his fellows and stepped beside a tree so that he could better see the riders' approach. They came into view soon enough, rounding a bend at the base of the hill. Twenty knights trotted along the rutted roadway, their armour painfully dull, their banner hanging limply from its pole. Pathetic, thought Alandriakh.

The Dark Elves waited until the knights had almost passed before pivoting their machines upon their target. Alandriakh brought his arm down as the command to fire and the air was filled with hissing bolts. The shouts of men and the whinny of horses greeted the fusillade, which scythed down half a dozen knights with the first salvo. The survivors were thrown into anarchy by the surprise attack, their horses rearing, the riders' bellowing to each other in confusion. More bolts quickly silenced them and soon the road was littered with armoured corpses and the bloodied remains of their steeds.

Alandriakh watched as a few of the knights struggled to rise despite their wounds, while others crawled desperately for the cover of their comrades' bodies. He drew a curved dagger from his belt and set off down the hill. Perhaps Khaine smiled on him after all.

HARPIES

In the city of Karond Kar, Dark Elves can pay witness to a bloody spectacle that fills them with elation and fear in equal measure. Upon the thermals of the sacrificial pyres soar the Harpies – winged beasts with a savage beauty. Some claim they are the souls of slain Witch Elves given form, others that they are a manifestation of Khaine. They are certainly vicious enough for either to be true.

They are creatures similar in temperament to the Dark Elves, that is for sure, for flocks of Harpies delight in tormenting their victims and feast upon raw flesh. In Dark Elf lore, Harpies are considered to be a sign of good fortune and it is claimed that if they ever deserted Karond Kar, the city would fall to the enemy within ninety days.

	M	WS	BS	S	T	W	I	A	LD
Harpy	5	3	0	3	3	1	5	2	6

Special Rules
Flying unit.

Beasts: Harpies are not Dark Elves, and thus are beneath consideration by the Druchii. Harpies never cause Panic tests to friendly units. They cannot be affected by a Cauldron of Blood either.

COLD ONES

Cold Ones are an ancient race of green-skinned reptiles that live in the dark caves and tunnels in the mountains underneath Hag Graef. Their cold flesh is almost immune to pain and their bodies exude a toxic slime. Dark Elves can withstand small quantities of this slime and tiny amounts are used to make the poisons and intoxicating brews used by the Assassins and Witch Elves of Khaine.

Though single-minded when hunting and feeding, Cold Ones are extremely stubborn beasts, and not at all intelligent. It takes great strength, practice and willpower to master such a steed, and those Dark Elves that do so earn fear, if not respect, from their fellow Naggarothi nobles.

	M	WS	BS	S	T	W	I	A	LD
Cold One	7	3	0	4	4	1	2	1	3

Special Rules
Fear, Stupidity.

Thick-skinned: Due to their thick hides, Cold Ones give a +2 bonus to their rider's saving throw instead of the normal +1 save given to cavalry models.

DARK PEGASUS

The Dark Elves trap and enslave a wide range of strange creatures from the Chaos Wastes and amongst these is the feral Dark Pegasus. These beasts fly south to make their nests on the most northern peaks of the Iron Mountains, and from these the Dark Elves steal their young – a fully-grown Dark Pegasus is too savage to be trained. The majority of these young Dark Pegasi are taken to the city of Ghrond, for they are favoured as steeds by the Sorceresses of the Dark Convent.

A Dark Pegasus moves swiftly upon its bat-like wings and is able to patiently soar above the mountains, shadowing its quarry for hours at a time. When it spots an opportunity to attack, it folds its wings and drops into a swooping dive, directing its long horn towards its target to impale it with deadly precision.

	M	WS	BS	S	T	W	I	A	LD
Dark Pegasus	8	3	0	4	4	3	4	2	6

Special Rules
Fly.

Impale Attack: The Dark Pegasus attacks with +1 Strength when it charges into combat.

DARK STEED

When the armies of Nagarythe invaded the rest of Ulthuan, they captured many of the famous horses of Ellyrion. The finest of all Elven steeds, these beasts were taken back to Anlec, and there they were bred with the native horses and corrupted with Dark Magic to turn them into black-flanked killers. No longer truly a horse, a Dark Steed can outrun the steeds of other races, galloping for days without tiring. When Malekith was cast out of Ulthuan by the Sundering, many of these steeds were slain, but a few were taken upon the Black Arks. In the dark, chill forests of Naggarond, the Druchii had their slaves cut pastureland for their mounts, and flogged thousands of slaves to death to till the soil for food to give their prized creatures. The Dark Steeds fed upon the bones and flesh of fallen captives, so that dead slaves were as useful as living ones. However, no sooner had the number of Dark Steeds begun to flourish than the Cold Ones were discovered in the Underworld Sea and the nobles of Naggarond chose to abandon their old mounts in favour of the new bestial reptiles of the caves. These days, Dark Steeds are almost exclusively used by Dark Riders to patrol ahead of the army, and by heralds and messengers as they ride from city to city.

	M	WS	BS	S	T	W	I	A	LD
Dark Steed	9	3	0	3	3	1	4	1	5

BLACK DRAGON

Dragons once ruled the skies of the world, before the coming of the Old Ones. These majestic reptiles soared across the icy plains and upon the thermals of prehistoric volcanoes, the kings of the air. Now, their race is but a shadow of its former power and majesty. When the Old Ones arrived, the greatest Dragons found the world too warm for their liking and hid from the bright sun, while more still stole into caverns and the ocean deeps with the coming of Chaos.

These massive beasts slumber still, undisturbed by the passing millennia, all but impossible to rouse. Younger Dragons, still tremendously powerful monsters, sometimes rise from their sleep at the call of the Elves, or when other events disturb their aeons-long dreams. Most of these rest in the realm of Caledor on Ulthuan, friends to the Dragon Princes who are descended from the great archmage Caledor Dragontamer, ally of Aenarion.

Like all intelligent creatures, Dragons are prone to acts of good or ill depending upon their nature and upbringing. When Malekith began his plotting to usurp the Phoenix Crown, his agents stole Dragon eggs from their nests in Caledor. These were secretly nurtured in Nagarythe by Malekith, and enchanted with dark spells to corrupt the unborn Dragons within. The fiercest Black Dragon from this first clutch was Sulekh, the

mount of the Witch King. Since Sulekh's death at the hands of the High Elves, Sulekh's children have continued to fight ferociously alongside the Dark Elves, in revenge for their slain ancestor.

A Black Dragon is capable of slaughtering armies with its claws, horns and fangs. With expulsions of noxious gas from its maw, it can wither the lungs of its victims and desiccate their flesh. The thick hide of a Black Dragon protects it from even the fiercest blows of its enemies. Perhaps the greatest weapon of all is the overwhelming wyrm-dread that fills the enemy upon sighting such a bloodthirsty and destructive monster.

	M	WS	BS	S	T	W	I	A	LD
Black Dragon	6	6	0	6	6	6	3	5	8

Special Rules
Fly, Terror, Large Target, 3+ Scaly Skin.

Noxious Breath: A Black Dragon has a breath weapon attack. Hits are resolved at Strength 4 and any unit taking casualties from the noxious breath must pass a Leadership test with a -3 modifier in order to declare charges in their next Movement phase. Units that are Immune to Psychology take damage as normal but do not suffer any additional effects.

MALEKITH'S DRAGON RIDERS

Seraphon is the terrifying Black Dragon that the Witch King rides to battle.

After a band of Shades found a clutch of unguarded eggs, deep within the Spiteful Peaks mountain range, Malekith ordered that the eggs be brought back to Naggarond. There they were ritually tended by the priestesses of Khaine for almost a century until they hatched. Seraphon was the first to emerge and before the Witch Elves could stop him, he had destroyed many of the other eggs. Malekith was impressed by the Dragon's ruthless instincts and decided that he would take the Dragon as his own mount.

The few remaining Dragon hatchlings were all given to Malekith's most favoured generals. These nobles have spent many decades training to fight with these monstrous beasts in preparation for the Witch King's next assault on Ulthuan.

Now Malekith feels the time is right for his people to wage war once again. The Witch King and Seraphon will fight at the fore of a highly trained flight of Black Dragons, whose surprise strike attacks will ravage the shores of the Old World and the cities of Ulthuan.

WAR HYDRA

Nobody is sure of the origins of the Hydras – whether they were creatures of the world before the Old Ones came, or are some offspring of Chaos brought about by the warping effects of the Winds of Magic. They first came into the armies of the Naggarothi from the magical Annulii Mountains on Ulthuan, and can be found throughout the Iron and Black Spine ranges in Naggaroth. Since the start of the civil war, the Dark Elves have trained War Hydras to break the lines of enemy troops with their massive bulk and fiery breath. In vast dungeons beneath the cities, Beastmasters continually experiment with different breeding techniques and cast enchantments upon the Hydra's eggs to raise the ferocity of successive generations to new heights.

The War Hydra is a titanic monster, bred especially for their enormous size and ferocious temperament from creatures captured from the caverns below the Blackspine Mountains. They are all fearsome beasts with thick, uniquely-patterned scales, and have many serpentine heads that belch smoke and fire and rend men with their sharp fangs, or coil their necks about the bodies of their victims and crush the life from their prey.

	M	WS	BS	S	T	W	I	A	LD
War Hydra	6	4	0	5	5	5	2	7	6
Beastmaster	6	4	4	3	3	1	5	2	8

Beastmaster's Scourge

The Beastmasters of Karond Kar use vicious whips and goads to train and steer their monstrous creatures, and the pain they inflict is enough for even the brutish beasts they lead into battle to feel.

Hand weapon. In addition, all the wielder's close combat attacks are Armour Piercing.

Special Rules

Eternal Hatred, Monster and Handlers, Terror, Large Target, 4+ Scaly Skin, Regenerate.

Fiery Breath: The War Hydra has a flaming breath weapon attack. The Strength of this attack is equal to the War Hydra's remaining Wounds.

Beastmasters: The bulk of the War Hydra makes a great shield for the Beastmasters that drive it, protecting them from arrows and other missiles. When hits would normally be randomised between the models of a unit, such as for shooting or a spell, such hits are not allocated randomly but instead are all resolved against the War Hydra. In close combat, the Beastmasters are adept at using the bulk of the Hydra to protect themselves, so all enemies that can choose to attack them or the Hydra must allocate their attacks against the Hydra.

If the Beastmasters are killed, the War Hydra must make a Monster Reaction test just like a ridden monster that loses its rider. When calculating victory points, the Beastmasters are always ignored – assume that the Hydra was fighting on its own as a one-model unit.

Only the Beastmasters themselves have the skill to control such a ferocious beast. Therefore, no other model may join a War Hydra unit.

ANATH RAEMA

Anath Raema is the sister of Khaine, and is the goddess of the savage hunt. It is from Anath Raema that Dark Elves are gifted the joy of the chase and the thrill of the kill. It matters not to Anath Raema who or what is hunted, for every living creature is seen as mere prey to this bloodthirsty goddess.

Anath Raema wears a belt of heads and hands of hunters who benefited from her blessings and did not praise her in return. Her amorous advances were spurned by Kurnous, and so she is also worshipped by some Elves as a patron of jealous lovers; an avenging deity who will hunt down and slay those who have wronged her supplicants.

MANTICORE

Dark Elves hold no creature in higher esteem than the Manticore, for they believe it is one of the thousand incarnations of their most powerful god, Khaine. Born amidst the warping energies of the Chaos Wastes, Manticores have the body of a gigantic lion, larger than any of the predators of the mountains. They fly upon wings like those of a huge bat, and have whip-like tails tipped with a vicious barb. A single strike of this poisoned spur can fell even the toughest warrior.

Once fully-grown, Manticores fly south, to where they reign supreme in the Iron Mountains, hunting lions, bears and other dangerous beasts. Manticores are the fiercest, most aggressive creature in the world, and will attack anything that they perceive as food or a threat. Occasionally a Hydra, Chymera, Basilisk or other monstrous interloper will stray onto a Manticore's territory, with cataclysmic consequences. The valleys and peaks echo to the roars and hisses of the battling monsters, causing avalanches and landslides. The two beasts rend skin and flesh, goring and biting each other with titanic ferocity.

The Manticore is usually the victor, having ripped the head bloodily from its foe, or stabbed it repeatedly with its poisoned tail. The Manticore will then drag the bloodied carcass of its defeated enemy back to its lair, to feast and restore its spent strength.

Manticores are highly prized as mounts, despite their immensely ferocious nature. Particularly daring Dark Elves, usually from the Shades clan, venture into the Iron Mountains and as far north as the Chaos Wastes in search of young Manticores to bring back to the cities of the Dark Elves. Many of these expeditions do not return, either slain by the elements, or torn apart by the creatures that they hunt.

Though wild and dangerous, Manticores can be tamed enough to take a rider, though they remain highly feral. Even if his monstrous steed occasionally ignores his commands and pitches him into unfavourable fights, a Dark Elf considers this a minor risk compared to the fear and respect that having such a mount brings.

	M	WS	BS	S	T	W	I	A	LD
Manticore	6	5	0	5	5	4	5	4	5

Special Rules
Fly, Terror, Large Target, Killing Blow.

Uncontrollable: At the start of each friendly turn, a model riding a Manticore must pass a Leadership test to control its mount. If the test is failed, the Manticore and its rider are subject to Frenzy until the start of their next turn. Also, should a Manticore's rider be slain, the Manticore is automatically affected by the 'Raaargh!' Monster Reaction result, with no Leadership test or D6 roll.

HEKARTI

It was to Hekarti that Morathi first turned when she set out upon the long path to mastering sorcery. Hekarti is a goddess of conjurations and Dark Magic and from her the wizards of the Dark Elves draw much of their power. She has no shrine, save perhaps a small temple in the Dark Convent in Ghrond, for Hekarti is said to be everywhere. She is many-headed, like the Hydra, so that she can see all of the winds of magic, and has six-arms to carry her sacred accoutrements; a serpent-headed staff, a beating heart, a scorpion, a broken arrow, a serrated dagger and a phial of orphan's tears.

With Hekarti's favour it is possible to tap directly into the Winds of Magic and unleash their full power. Such is the nature of Dark Elf sorcery, making their spells far more destructive than those of lesser races. Hekarti does not give her blessing for free though, and there is always a price to pay, in blood -- the Sorceress's or someone else's, Hekarti cares not!

COMMANDERS

The so-called noble-born rulers of Naggaroth range from sycophantic schemers to masterful strategists that have waged war across a hundred battlefields. They are selfish individuals, their arrogance matched only by their martial prowess. Druchii lords wear the finest suits of armour and carry a lethal assortment of blades with which they carve a bloody path through their hated foes. Dark Elf nobles command the lower classes that comprise their armies through fear and bloodshed. Amongst the lower-born Druchii it is viewed as better to die at the hands of an enemy on the battlefield than to face the wrath of a disappointed Dark Elf lord.

The lives of Dark Elves are sustained by the misery they can inflict on others and their own offspring are no exception. Those striplings that survive to adulthood are sent on a yearlong raiding expedition. It is a chance for the Dark Elf to prove his ruthlessness and establish his reputation. Dark Elves abhor weakness and those found wanting are easy prey for rivals with ambition. No Dark Elf attains rank, or retains it for long, unless he is utterly without mercy. In this way only the strongest and most ruthless survive for any duration.

The Druchii are a murderous race and the risk of an Assassin's blade is a constant threat. To alleviate their paranoia, a rigid code of etiquette has evolved. The lowborn classes may not approach within three sword lengths of a noble without being summoned. A retainer may stand as close as two sword lengths whilst a trusted retainer, such as a lieutenant or bodyguard, may stand just outside a single sword's length. The closest, most intimate space is reserved for lovers, playthings and mortal foes. A Dark Elf lord is well within his rights to execute any who disregard this code.

Many Dreadlords owe their positions of power to their bloodlines, cruel and dashing exploits or favour at Malekith's court. Others are granted temporary power by means of a writ of iron – an edict granted by one of the six rulers of the great cities of Naggaroth or, occasionally, by the Witch King himself. A Dark Elf with a writ carries the power and authority of his sponsor and any who question the iron edict are subject to the wrath of his patron. Should a Druchii fail in his appointed task or show cowardice whilst acting in their sponsor's name, the writ is melted down and the molten remains poured down the noble's throat. Such is the price of failure in Naggaroth.

	M	WS	BS	S	T	W	I	A	LD
Dreadlord	5	7	6	4	3	3	8	4	10
Master	5	6	6	4	3	2	7	3	9

Special Rules
Eternal Hatred.

MENGIL MANHIDE

Even amongst the Dark Elves of Naggaroth, Mengil of Clar Karond is particularly noted for his bloodthirsty nature. While most Dark Elves would happily slit the throat of any who got in their way, Mengil kills for the fun of it, without care or thought of consequences.

Mengil's father was a powerful lord, and set his many sons tasks in order to weed out those he deemed too weak to carry his bloodline. In one such test, a powerful Norseman was released into the Black Forests. The young Mengil was sent to hunt this human, to return with proof of success, or not at all. Mengil tracked his quarry through the icy wilderness, eventually overcoming his more powerful foe with speed and skill. Mengil smeared blood across his face and drank deeply from the heart of his fallen enemy, before flaying the skin from the Norseman. Mengil wore the bloodied skin as a cloak as he walked back into Clar Karond, earning him the respect of his father and the honorific title 'Manhide'. He went on to spread terror across the Old World as captain of the renowned Manflayers regiment.

ASSASSINS

While young Dark Elf girls taken by Khaine become Witch Elves, male children raised in the temples of Khaine are destined to be Assassins. These are the most deadly and evil Dark Elves of all, masters of subtle and murderous magic. The neophytes are raised in the blood fields of the temples, learning the arts of war and death. The merciless and deadly few that survive the first ten years of this training, killing their fellow adepts in face-to-face fighting or by more devious means, go to the great temples of Naggarond and Har Ganeth, where they learn the deepest mysteries of Khaine. None outside the cult know all of the secrets of the temples, save perhaps Hellebron and Shadowblade, and each Assassin will learn the particular skills and techniques of his master.

The cult of Khaine hires out the services of its Assassins to Malekith and the other rulers of Naggarond, in exchange for sacrifices, wealth and political favour. Though the price is high, such is the skill of these killers that there is a constant demand for their services. Many Assassins ply their deadly trade in the cities of the Dark Elves, eliminating their employer's competitors and aiding in coups against the ruling families. Some Assassins are hired by Black Ark commanders, to train their Corsairs in war and to sow terror amongst the populace of their raid's target.

Assassins are also employed to keep discipline and loyalty amongst the troops of an army captain. The skill and guile of these deadly warriors is such that the troops they accompany usually do not know that there is an Assassin within their ranks. The fear and uncertainty this causes helps to keep seditious talk and rebellion to a minimum, for no Dark Elf can be absolutely certain with whom he is conspiring.

Assassins are masters of using poison and coat their weapons with a variety of venoms – some of which are deadly, others which paralyse or stupefy their victim so that they can be captured and tortured for information or pleasure. One scratch from some of these poisons is enough to send a man into agonising paroxysms as his nerves burn, his heart explodes or his bones crack and shatter. The Assassins take great pleasure in the awful demises of their victims, and are adept at keeping prisoners alive for many days. Often they can extract confessions and information from captives much more quickly than the crude tortures used by other Naggarothi interrogators.

	M	WS	BS	S	T	W	I	A	LD
Assassin	5	9	9	4	3	2	10	3	10

Special Rules
Eternal Hatred, Khainite, Always Strikes First, Poisoned Attacks, Scout.

Hidden: An Assassin is a special type of character. He begins the game hidden in one of the following units: Dark Elf Spearmen, Dark Elf Crossbowmen, Black Ark Corsairs, Shades, Witch Elves, Har Ganeth Executioners, or Black Guard of Naggarond. Make a note of which unit the Assassin is hiding in.

A hidden Assassin is not placed on the table during deployment, but is revealed later in the game. If his concealing unit is wiped out or flees from the battlefield before he is revealed, the Assassin is also lost and counts as a casualty. There is no other way the Assassin can be harmed before he is revealed.

Hidden Assassins may be revealed at the beginning of any of your turns, or at the start of any Close Combat phase. Declare that the unit contains an Assassin and place the model in the front rank. Displace a rank-and-file model to make room for the Assassin. If the unit is in close combat, the Assassin displaces any rank-and-file model in the unit that is in contact with the enemy. If there are no rank-and-file models to displace in a suitable position, a command model or character must be moved to make room for the Assassin.

A Killer not a Leader: Although Assassins are character models, units in the Dark Elf army may not use an Assassin's Leadership and an Assassin can never be chosen to be your army's General.

SORCERESSES

Elves are magical beings with a natural affinity for guiding and channelling the shifting winds of magic that stream from the Realm of Chaos. In the ancient days of their race, the Elves learnt the secrets of manipulating this mystical power from the Slann, the most powerful servants of the ancient creators known as the Old Ones. Steeped in magical lore, the Elves honed their powers in the long wars against the Daemon hordes that attacked their realm after the coming of Chaos.

For all the control and expertise of the Elven mages of old, there was always a limit to the amount of power they could harness – the risk of madness, daemonic attack and spiritual corruption prevented the Elves from delving deeper into the power of Chaos. The first of the Elves to venture into this forbidden territory was Morathi, the mother of the Witch King. With dark rituals and bloody sacrifices, she wielded the raw power of Chaos, moulding it to her bidding. Morathi used sorcery – the unrefined power of magic – to cast enchantments of foretelling and spells of destruction.

When Nagarythe raised war against the other realms of Ulthuan, Morathi had already corrupted several of the Mages of Saphery. Tempted by the power of sorcery, they turned against their fellow wizards and magical war raged. Eventually, the sorcerers were forced to flee, and sought protection and tutelage from Morathi and Malekith. To this day, Dark Elves study the sorcerous arts, seeking to increase their power and influence.

Chief amongst the wizards of Naggaroth are the 'sisters' of the Dark Convent of Sorceresses, who are gathered in the great fortress of Ghrond. Competition for positions in the Dark Convent are bloody and fierce, and only the most powerful and ruthless Sorceresses survive the initiations. Those that succeed learn some of the most powerful magic in the world. They can call upon ancient daemonic entities to devour their enemies, hurl storms of wicked shards at their foes or engulf them with bolts of dark energy. Most significantly, sorcery allows a wizard to tap into an almost limitless supply of magical energy to fuel their spells when the Winds of Magic blow fitfully.

	M	WS	BS	S	T	W	I	A	LD
Supreme Sorceress	5	4	4	3	3	3	5	1	9
Sorceress	5	4	4	3	3	2	5	1	8

A Dark Elf Wizard knows spells from the Lore of Dark Magic or one of the following Lores from Warhammer: Fire, Shadow, Metal or Death. In addition, they all know the *Power of Darkness* spell. See over the page for details of Dark Magic.

Special Rules
Eternal Hatred.

Druchii Sorcery: Dark Elf Wizards may use any number of power dice to cast spells, they are not limited by their magic level like other Wizards.

THE PROPHECY OF DEMISE

"Though will it come to pass that the firstborn son of noble blood shall rise to power. The child will be learned in the darkest arts and he will raise an army of terrible beasts. Thus will the Dark King fall, slain by neither blade nor arrow but by a sorcerous power of darkest magic and so shall his body be consumed in the flames and for all eternity burn."

As Aenarion drew the Blade of Khaine, Caledor was gifted with a prophecy that spoke of the tragedy that would befall Elvenkind. Part of the prophecy talks of a great warrior cast from his home by a sorcerer, and Malekith believes it is he to whom the prophecy refers. As a result, male Dark Elf wizards are regarded with disdain, fear and superstition, and they cannot be admitted to the Dark Convent. There are those in Naggaroth, however, who will employ such sorcerers to avoid owing a debt to the Convent of Sorceresses.

THE LORE OF DARK MAGIC

To randomly generate a spell from the Lore of Dark Magic, roll a D6 and consult the chart below. If you roll the same spell twice, roll again. Any Sorceress can swap one spell for Chillwind.

D6	Spell	Difficulty		D6	Spell	Difficulty
1	Chillwind	5+		4	Blade Wind	8+
2	Doombolt	6+		5	Soul Stealer	10+
3	Word of Pain	7+		6	Black Horror	11+

Chillwind Cast on 5+
Calling upon the coldness of Nagaelythe of the Utterdark, the Dark Elf unleashes a freezing wind against her enemies.

Magic missile, 24" range, D6 S4 hits, any unit taking casualties cannot shoot in its next turn.

Doombolt Cast on 6+
As the invocation is spoken, the other-worldly beast known as Kharaidon unleashes a bolt of pure darkness upon the Dark Elves' adversaries.

Magic missile, 18" range, D6 S5 hits.

Word of Pain Cast on 7+
Upon uttering the true name of the Serpent Lord, an unnatural and unbearable agony suffuses the body of the caster's hated foes.

Target one enemy unit within 24". *Word of Pain* may be cast into close combat. Until the start of the caster's next Magic phase, all models in the affected unit have their WS and BS reduced to 1.

Bladewind Cast On 8+
With a plea to the Mistress of a Thousand Cuts, the Dark Elf Sorceress conjures up a storm of magical swords with which to assail the enemy.

Target one enemy unit visible to the caster within 24". The spell inflicts 3D6 WS4, S4 close combat attacks upon the target. One of these attacks can be allocated against each character and champion in the unit.

Soul Stealer Cast on 10+
The Daemon-crawler Anchan-Rogar reaches out from his domain and plucks the souls from the enemy.

Target one enemy unit within 12", which may be in close combat. Every model in the unit takes a S2 hit, with no armour saves allowed. Each unsaved wound caused adds 1 Wound to the caster (but cannot take the sorceress above double her starting Wounds).

Black Horror Cast on 11+
The sorceress conjures a whirling vortex of devastating magical energy that drags her victims into one of the infernal regions.

Place the centre of the large template anywhere within 18" of the caster. All models touched by the template must pass a Strength test or suffer a Wound, no armour saves allowed. Any unit that suffers one or more Wounds must immediately test for Panic.

EXTRA SPELL – Power of Darkness
All Dark Elf wizards know the Power of Darkness spell in addition to their other spells.

Power of Darkness Cast on 4+
The raw energy of magic can be immensely powerful, but it is highly unstable and can be as dangerous to the wielder as it is to the foe.

If *Power of Darkness* is successfully cast, the wizard immediately gains D3+1 extra power dice. These dice are added to those available to the sorceress, but keep them separate or use different-coloured dice. These additional dice cannot be used to dispel spells in play or be stored from turn-to-turn in any way possible. For each of these dice still unused at the end of the Magic phase, the sorceress suffers a Strength 4 hit.

MALEKITH, THE WITCH KING

Malekith is the son of Morathi and Aenarion. He grew to be a mighty warrior, a great sorcerer and a brilliant general, but was shunned by his folk when Aenarion was slain. When Bel-Shanaar was chosen to rule in his stead, Malekith began a long campaign to regain his rightful throne – a campaign that has lasted for five thousand years.

Now reigning over his dispossessed people as the Witch King of Naggaroth, Malekith is a fearsome warrior and mighty sorcerer. With both spell and blade he destroys all that oppose him. His burnt and scarred body is bound within the protective plates of the Armour of Midnight, and few face the wrath of the Witch King and survive.

	M	WS	BS	S	T	W	I	A	LD
Malekith	5	8	6	5	4	3	8	4	10

Equipment
Malekith is armed and armoured with the following magic items: Destroyer, the Armour of Midnight, the Circlet of Iron and the Spellshield.

Magic
Malekith is a Level 4 Wizard and knows spells from the Lore of Dark Magic.

Mount
Malekith may ride a Cold One, his Black Dragon Seraphon (use the normal profile given on page 57) or the Black Chariot. The Black Chariot is a Cold One Chariot with a 2+ armour save (see page 53).

Magic items
Destroyer (Magic weapon).
Forged by the Witch King of Naggaroth himself, as a powerful symbol of the Dark Elves' determination to destroy the High Elves, Destroyer is ensorcelled to steal a foe's magic. It has been the bane of hundreds of heroes and wizards from all the races of the world – but especially the High Elves.

In every round of close combat, if Malekith hits a foe carrying magic items or who can cast spells, Destroyer will destroy a power on a D6 roll of 4+. Roll once immediately, not per hit. The enemy model loses one level of magic (and one random spell), or one randomly determined magic item. If the target has both items and spells, roll a D6: 1-3: take a magic level, 4-6: take a magic item. Once this has been resolved, roll to wound as normal.

Armour of Midnight (Magic armour)
Malekith's armour is forged from the hardest meteoric iron and covered in runes that protect the Witch King against any mortal weapon.

Heavy armour. 2+ ward save against non-magical attacks. Malekith can never suffer more than one wound from a single attack, so attacks that do multiple wounds or kill outright only ever inflict a single wound.

Spellshield (Magic armour)
The Spellshield is inscribed with a rune that absorbs mystical power and then unleashes this captured energy back at the enemy.

Shield. Magic resistance (2). If a spell cast at Malekith is dispelled by a dispel roll, the caster suffers a Strength 6 hit for every dice used to cast the spell. For Bound Items, the Spellshield inflicts one Strength 6 hit.

Circlet of Iron (Arcane item)
The Circlet of Iron is said to be older even than the Elves and is a potent source of magical power.

Malekith gains one extra power dice in the Dark Elves' Magic phase (which only he may use) and he also generates one extra dispel dice for his army in the opponent's Magic phase.

Special Rules
Eternal Hatred, Immune to Psychology.

Absolute Power: If Malekith is included in your army, then he must be the General. Any unit in Malekith's army that is within 12" of him automatically passes all panic tests.

MORATHI, THE HAG SORCERESS

After the Witch King himself, Morathi is the single most powerful Dark Elf in all of Naggaroth. Born to scheming and politics, and a talented Sorceress, Morathi has spent five thousand years teaching her son all she knows of statecraft and magic, and works to maintain his grip on the throne of Naggaroth. Morathi is totally dedicated to her son, as he is to her, and though some would say their relationship is unnatural, between them they rule Naggaroth with an iron grip and bloodied sword.

Morathi has always had the taint of Chaos about her – she met Malekith's father, Aenarion, when the Elven lord rescued her from a Chaos attack. Many believe that it was during her time as a captive that the insidious claws of the Dark Gods first crept into her soul. It was Morathi who founded the Cult of Pleasure on Ulthuan, which eventually led to bloody civil war and the cataclysm of the Sundering. Morathi was the first to perfect the Dark Art, opening up gateways to the Realm of Chaos to steal vast and unimaginable powers. Combined with her stunning beauty and keen intellect, it is Morathi's magical abilities that allow her to hold sway over her enemies.

Over the millennia, Morathi has struck daemonic pacts with many vile and disturbing forces, and can unleash the terrible power of Chaos with barely a thought. She is capable of the most powerful magic possible, and some believe it has long been her plan to destroy Ulthuan's magical vortex in order to unleash the Realm of Chaos upon the world.

	M	WS	BS	S	T	W	I	A	LD
Morathi	5	5	4	3	3	3	6	3	10
Sulephet	8	4	0	4	4	3	4	3	6

Equipment
Hand weapon and either Heartrender or the Darksword. Morathi may also be given one Arcane Item and one Enchanted Item from the Magic Items listed on pages 100-103.

Mount
Morathi rides her Dark Pegasus Sulephet.

Special Rules
Eternal Hatred, Druchii Sorcery (see page 62).

Thousand and One Dark Blessings: Morathi has magic resistance (2) and a 4+ ward save.

Enchanting Beauty: Any model in base contact with Morathi at the start of the Close Combat phase must pass a Leadership test or is reduced to Weapon Skill 1 until the end of the phase.

The First Sorceress: Morathi is a Level 4 Wizard and knows *all* of the spells from the Lore of Dark Magic. In addition, Morathi adds +1 to all casting rolls.

Magic Items
Heartrender (Magic weapon)
Such is Morathi's skill with the lance-like Heartrender that she can pluck a victim's heart from his chest with a single, well-placed blow.

Lance. On the turn she charges, Morathi gains the Killing Blow rule.

The Darksword (Magic weapon)
A sword forged with spells of blinding and enfeeblement incanted in the Dark Tongue by an evil sorcerer. A foe struck by this weapon will be horribly weakened, even if he survives his wounds.

Hand weapon. Each wound inflicted on an enemy character or champion (after saves, etc) also deducts 1 from the model's S, A and T for the remainder of the game. If any of these is reduced to 0 the enemy is removed as a casualty.

CRONE HELLEBRON

Of all the Hag Queens, Hellebron is the most ancient, save only the mother of the Witch King, Morathi, the first of the brides of Khaine. But while the youth and beauty of Morathi is eternally renewed, that of Hellebron is now almost expended. The power of the blood no longer refreshes this ancient Hag Queen as it once did. Each year more sacrifices are needed to fill the cauldron, and yet the rejuvenating effects last for less and less time. Once beautiful beyond measure, Hellebron must now endure many dark months as an old and ugly crone for each day of renewed youth.

Still, ugly and worn as she may be, Hellebron is the greatest of the brides of Khaine. Witch Elves kneel before her to take the rites of the god of murder. To entertain their mistress, the youngest she-Elves dance upon the steps of Khaine's altars, whilst Hellebron and the lesser Hags feast upon flesh and sate their withering lust for warm blood. They are the leaders and mistresses of the Witch Elves, with memories of battles and bloodletting that span five thousand years.

As leader of the cult of Khaine, Hellebron rules over the city of Har Ganeth. As well as a horde of frenzied Witch Elves, Hellebron can call upon the deadly Executioners of that city, and also raise the populace to arms with promises of Khaine's favour and threats of his bloody

displeasure. Hellebron leads this army to battle when flushed with magical youth from the Cauldron of Blood, while the Hag Queen prefers to cloister herself in the great temple of Khaine during her long months of decrepit suffering.

	M	WS	BS	S	T	W	I	A	LD
Hellebron	5	7	6	4	3	3	9	4	10

Equipment
Hellebron carries the Deathsword, the Parrying Blade and the Amulet of Fire. She may accompany a Cauldron of Blood.

Gifts of Khaine
Hellebron has the following Gifts of Khaine (see page 99): **Rune of Khaine, Cry of War and Witchbrew.**

Magic Items
Deathsword (Magic weapon).
The blade of this long, black sword glistens with dark magic. When it is wielded in combat, the sharp tip of the sword leaves a gleaming red trail in the air.

Hits from the Deathsword are resolved at Strength 10.

Parrying Blade (Magic weapon)
Moving with a life of its own, the Parrying Blade deflects the attacks of the enemy.

One model in base contact chosen by the Dark Elves player, or the Hellebron's opponent in a challenge, loses one Attack (to a minimum of 1). See Hand of Khaine on page 99 for the full rules.

Amulet of Fire (Talisman)
This amulet wreaths its wearer in a mystical flame that deflects magical energy.

The first spell cast against Hellebron or her unit in each Magic phase is dispelled on a D6 roll of 4+. This is rolled after any other dispel attempts.

Special Rules
Eternal Hatred, Khainite, Frenzy.

Two magic weapons: Hellebron is armed with two magic weapons. She benefits from the effects of both and, as long as she fights on foot, this also grants her +1 Attack in close combat, just like models fighting with two normal hand weapons.

Queen of Khaine: Even if Hellebron is not the General, all Khainite units in the army treat Hellebron as the army General for Leadership tests – they may not use the Leadership of the normal army General.

As noted in the army list, if Hellebron *is* your General, you may take Witch Elves as Core units rather than as Special units.

MALUS DARKBLADE

The tale of Malus Darkblade is one of greed, treachery and much bloodshed. Born of one of the noble families of Hag Graef, Malus is cruel, ruthless and cunning. Above all these things, he is ambitious and craves power. Thus, Malus sought out an ancient magical treasure, but in discovering it, he also found something far older and more terrible.

Malus was possessed by the Daemon Tz'arkan. His life and soul were forfeit and he had but one way of escaping his fate – to find five artefacts of power that could be used in a ritual to free Tz'arkan for eternity and restore Malus' soul. He had only a year to succeed. Such was Malus' determination and ruthlessness that he slew his own father for possession of one of the artefacts needed for his salvation.

Upon the eve of his doom, Malus returned to the place of his possession and performed the ritual, but Tz'arkan had tricked the Dark Elf lord. Upon escaping from Malus' body, the treacherous Daemon took his soul as well. Caught between life and death, the soulless Malus wandered the Chaos Wastes for a decade, fighting and killing for others. Malus is a natural leader and his skills as a general have impressed even the Witch King. Armed with the Warpsword of Khaine, the only artefact not destroyed in the ritual to free himself, Malus was unstoppable. Eventually the merciless Druchii retrieved his soul, but in the process the Daemon was once again imprisoned within Malus' body.

Malus can call upon Tz'arkan to imbue his body with unholy power, but the source of the Druchii's greatest strength is his limitless reservoir of hatred. Malus firmly believes that with hate, all things are possible. Now, after many years of journeying, Malus has returned to his home city of Hag Graef. None can foretell his true intentions, but he has lost none of his thirst for power!

	M	WS	BS	S	T	W	I	A	LD
Malus	5	6	5	4	3	2	7	3	9
Spite	7	3	0	4	4	1	2	2	4

Equipment
Malus Darkblade wears heavy armour and wields the Warpsword of Khaine.

Mount
Malus rides the Cold One, Spite.

Magic Items
Warpsword of Khaine (Magic weapon)
This is one of the five fabled treasures that Malus had to retrieve in his quest to rid himself of the Daemon that possesses him.

In close combat, Malus may re-roll failed rolls to wound. Enemy models may not take armour saves against wounds inflicted by the Warpsword of Khaine.

Special Rules
Eternal Hatred.

Not Just a Dumb Brute: Spite does not suffer from Stupidity and any unit of Cold One Knights including Spite (we know who is really in charge!) are also not subject to Stupidity.

Tz'arkan: At the start of any of his turns, Malus may unleash the power of the Daemon Tz'arkan. The following apply to Malus for the rest of the battle:

- Malus is subject to Frenzy.

- Malus gains +1 WS, +1 S, +2 T, +2 I and +1 Ld.

- If Malus is in base contact with a friendly model and not in contact with the enemy in any close combat phase, roll a D6. On a 1, 2 or 3 Tz'arkan's murderous rage drives Malus to attack his allies.

  Make Malus' normal attacks on a randomly determined model in base contact, resolved as if Malus were charging. Spite does not attack. The other model will strike back if it survives. No wounds carry over onto other models and no combat resolution is worked out.

SHADOWBLADE

Shadowblade is still young, being a mere 150 years old. His reputation, however, is already legendary. Stories of his grisly adventures are used as stories to scare Dark Elf children. His most famous exploit was the murder of the crew of a High Elf Hawkship, one by one, over a period of several days. Only the horribly mutilated captain was left alive, so that he could tell his kin of the mounting horror on the ship as the crew desperately attempted to corner Shadowblade – to no avail.

Shadowblade reports directly to Hellebron, and it is rumoured that she has used him to eliminate her Dark Elf political opponents. Such stories are difficult to substantiate, however, because no-one has seen Shadowblade's face and lived – he slew his master when he had learnt all that he could – and not even Hellebron knows what he looks like. What's more, those that start spreading such stories tend to come to a mysterious and untimely end...

	M	WS	BS	S	T	W	I	A	LD
Shadowblade	6	10	10	4	3	2	10	3	10

Equipment
Shadowblade has two hand weapons.

Gifts of Khaine
Shadowblade has the following Gifts of Khaine (see page 99): **Rending Stars, Dance of Doom, Touch of Death, Hand of Khaine and Dark Venom.**

Special Rules
Eternal Hatred, Khainite, A Killer Not a Leader (see page 61), Always Strikes First, Scout, Poisoned Attacks.

Master of Assassins: Shadowblade may use the Hidden rules of Assassins (page 61). Alternatively, he may be deployed on his own as a Scout. Lastly, he may attempt to hide inside the enemy army! After your opponent has deployed, secretly write down which enemy unit Shadowblade has attempted to infiltrate. This must be an infantry unit or war machine crew whose models are on 20mm or 25mm square bases. Shadowblade cannot join a unit of flyers.

The same rules for units being wiped out or fleeing (see page 61) apply to Shadowblade's concealing unit.

At the start of each of your opponent's turns after the first, roll a D6. On a roll of 2+ Shadowblade remains concealed. On a roll of a 1, the Master of Assassins has been discovered. Alternatively, Shadowblade may be revealed at the start of any of his turns after the first.

If Shadowblade was voluntarily revealed then the Dark Elf player may place him. If he was discovered then the opposing player places Shadowblade. If discovered, Shadowblade may make no attacks in the next close combat phase.

In either case, when Shadowblade is revealed, remove a normal rank-and-file member of the unit (he was killed before the battle), and place Shadowblade anywhere in contact with the unit. Both are now in close combat.

Magic Items
Potion of Strength (Enchanted item)
A potent magical brew created from Troll blood and the heart of a Griffon.

One use only. Shadowblade may drink this at the start of any close combat and it lasts until the start of the next player's turn. While it is in effect, the Potion of Strength grants +3 Strength.

Heart of Woe (Talisman)
The Heart of Woe is a large ruby that beats like a living heart. Should the bearer be slain, the crystal shatters into thousands of jagged shards, slaying those responsible for Shadowblade's death.

If Shadowblade is slain, centre a 5" circular template over his final position. Models completely covered are hit automatically, models partially under the template are hit on a D6 roll of 4+. The Heart of Woe inflicts a Strength 3 hit on affected models.

LOKHIR FELLHEART

Since his great-great-grandfather first fought in the Battle of the Waves, Lokhir's destiny has been set – to rule the *Tower of Blessed Dread* and prove his worth on the dangerous oceans. When Lokhir first took command he led his followers to an attack on the elven port of Tor Canabrae in the kingdom of Eataine. In the deepest winter the Black Ark and its fleet crept out of Karond Kar, shrouded by blizzards and storms. Bringing snows and lightning with them, Lokhir's warriors descended upon the town and razed it to the ground as a statement that the Fellhearts had returned.

When Lokhir's fame from the Tor Canabrae raid began to dwindle, he set out southwards in search of treasure with which to decorate the Fellheart palaces. Past Arnheim he sailed, leaving the High Elf colony to lesser raiders. Along the Vampire Coast he sailed, sinking ships crewed by the dead and fighting off boarding parties of rotted Zombies and animated Skeletons.

Lokhir's target was not the settlements of Pirate's Cove, nor the teeming temple-cities of the Lizardmen. He was intent upon the sunken city of Chupayotl in southern Lustria, the watery grave of the Old Ones' secrets. Lokhir led his fleet to the coast where the sunken city lay, and anchored his fleet above Chupayotl. With seven sorceresses hired from the Dark Convent, he cloaked his warriors with magic that allowed them to breath underwater. Thus protected, Lokhir led the most daring raid ever, on the drowned city of the ancients.

In the submerged ruins of the city, the Dark Elves battled with aquatic beasts. Gigantic squids and immense manta rays assailed them, and they fought amongst the jagged ruins against the disconcerting aquatic descendants of the ancient rulers of the jungle. Against this adversity, Lokhir triumphed, returning to the surface with chests laden with gold, magical artefacts that would fetch a high price in Ghrond, and ancient stone plaques containing the secrets of the Old Ones. His place in history had been sealed.

	M	WS	BS	S	T	W	I	A	LD
Lokhir Fellheart	5	6	6	4	3	2	7	3	9

Equipment
Lokhir Fellheart wears heavy armour, a sea dragon cloak (see page 45) and the Helm of the Kraken, and he also carries the Red Blades.

Magic Items
Helm of the Kraken (Enchanted item)
This golden helmet pre-dates the civilisation of the Elves, and was recovered by Lokhir Fellheart from the sunken ruins of Chupayotl off the southern coast of Lustria. It is fashioned in the likeness of a terrifying sea beast, and makes the bearer as resilient and dread-inspiring as its namesake.

The wearer gains Regeneration and causes Terror.

The Red Blades (Magic weapon)
When Lokhir Fellheart sacked the Temple of Gilgadresh, he took a statue made from Indan bloodsteel. Upon his return to Naggaroth, he had the metal forged into the deadliest pair of swords on the high seas.

A model wielding the Red Blades gains additional attacks in close combat equal to the number of ranks in the enemy unit he is attacking. In addition, he re-rolls failed rolls to Wound.

Special Rules
Eternal Hatred.

Daring Leap: At the start of any round of combat, before challenges are issued and impact hits are resolved, you may swap Lokhir with any other model in the same unit, as long as Lokhir is moved to a position that is in contact with the enemy. Lokhir may not use his heroic leap if he is in a challenge, or if he cannot move for any other reason.

Merciless Slaver: As long as Lokhir is alive, any unit that flees from close combat and is run down by Lokhir's unit is taken captive. Units destroyed in this way are worth double their normal amount of victory points, even if Lokhir and his unit are later destroyed.

KOURAN OF THE BLACK GUARD

	M	WS	BS	S	T	W	I	A	LD
Kouran	5	5	4	3	3	1	6	3	9

Equipment
Kouran wears the Armour of Grief and wields the Crimson Death (see page 101)).

Special Rules
Eternal Hatred.

Warrior Elite: Black Guard may re-roll any failed roll to hit in combat.

Captain of the Black Guard: The Black Guard unit including Kouran is Unbreakable.

Magic Item
The Armour of Grief (Magic Armour)
This enchanted armour was first worn by Arnaethron, one of the Witch King's first lieutenants during the Sundering. Those that attempt to strike the wearer must first overcome an aura of paralysing pain.

Heavy armour. Any model wishing to direct attacks against Kouran must first pass a Toughness test. If this is failed, the model may not make attacks in that round of combat. If the test is passed, the model may attack Kouran as normal. The test is taken just before any rolls to hit are made for the attacking model.

The longest-serving member of Malekith's Black Guard, Kouran has fought for the Witch King for nearly a thousand years. His rise to prominence was nothing short of meteoric, becoming Master of the Tower of Grief within his first decade of service. Kouran attained this vaunted position by slaying the previous incumbent, Diathenar, in a duel, choking the life out of his foe with Diathenar's own hair. Kouran had the flesh boiled from his rival's skull, which he keeps as a trophy.

Kouran then went on to fight across the world in the Witch King's armies, earning renown and infamy through his cruel exploits in the Empire, Bretonnia and Ind. Upon his triumphant return, Kouran sought out the Captain of the Black Guard, Khanaleth, and hurled him to a bone-splintering death from the east wall of Naggarond. Malekith, pleased with Kouran's ruthless nature, granted him command of the Black Guard, a position his has held for the last four hundred years – the corpses of seventeen challengers for his position now adorn the gates to the Tower of Grief.

Kouran is renowned for taking risks, though always claiming victory in the end. Once he sacrificed half of his army to draw the enemy into a trap, caring nothing for the lives of those who served him. He is an extremely efficient leader and is respected and feared by the Dark Elves under his command.

BATTLE OF THE BLOODY DAWN

Kouran staked his bloodiest claim to infamy when he led a host of Black Guard against Tor Anroc, capital of the Kingdom of Tiranoc. Deep is Kouran's loathing for this city, for it was the birthplace of hated Bel Shanaar.

The Black Guard attacked at night, preceded by bands of Shades who had dispatched the patrols and sentries. Unnoticed, the warriors of the Tower of Grief made their way along the spiralling road that led to the centre of the city. They struck without warning, cutting down the guards and forcing their way into the opulent palace. Tapestries burned and every portrait and ornament was slashed or smashed as the Black Guard tore through the building, exacting their master's revenge. Kouran's warriors hacked down all opposition and piled the corpses of their victims in the plaza in front of the palace. As the first rays of dawn joined the flames of the burning citadel, the Black Guard fought their way clear of the city. The new dawn revealed another atrocity, for the corpses of the Black Guard's foes had been arranged into one of the runes of Khaine, their departing spirits dedicated to the God of Murder.

TULLARIS OF HAR GANETH

Tullaris, captain of the Har Ganeth Executioners, is one of the most murderous leaders in the whole of Naggaroth. He once had all of the inhabitants of a captured town butchered and the town itself levelled to the ground simply because he didn't like its name! When Orcs of the Rusty Cleaver tribe tried to ambush Tullaris in the Badlands, he had the flesh boiled from their severed heads and used the skulls to decorate his palace in Har Ganeth. On Ulthuan he is known as Drakiur, the Dread-bringer, ever since he captured a band of Shadow Warriors near to the ruins of Anlec and had their body parts nailed to the eastern gate of the ancient citadel. His life has been punctuated by such bloody behaviour since he first heard the calling of Khaine.

Tullaris was but a young Elf when the first great sacrifice of Har Ganeth took place. As he looked up the bloody steps of the great temple, watching the heads of the High Elves bounce towards him, he felt the beckoning of Khaine in his blood. The next day he leapt up to the sacrificial dais, tore the blade from a guard's hand and slew his first captive, showering himself in his victim's blood. From that point on, his future was assured. He became one of the first of the sacred Executioners and spent every waking moment perfecting the art of slaying. So skilled did he become that he could slit the throats of five prisoners at once, all with a single blow. Hellebron took great interest in her talented new disciple, and when the Executioners first formed a bodyguard for the Hag Queen on a journey to Naggarond, she chose Tullaris to lead it.

While a loyal servant of Hellebron, Tullaris' devotion is to Khaine, and Khaine alone. He has slain fellow Executioners without flinching, if he thought that they were remiss in their dedication or showed sloppy blade work. Even the Witch Elves are wary of his anger, and no few of the brides of Khaine have found their necks upon Tullaris' chopping block.

Under his command, the Executioners have partaken in such cold-blooded destruction that they have gained a fearful reputation across the world. Beneath their banner, they march at the head of the army, eagerly seeking battle. Decapitating and eviscerating in a storm of blades, Tullaris' consecrated killers have slaughtered the best warriors their foes could offer. The merest rumour that they are part of an invading Dark Elf army can cause floods of refugees to flee before the Druchii forces and in battle, enemies rout rather than face Tullaris and his deadly warriors.

	M	WS	BS	S	T	W	I	A	LD
Tullaris	5	5	4	4	3	1	5	2	8

Equipment
Tullaris wears heavy armour and is armed with the Blade of Har Ganeth.

Special Rules
Eternal Hatred, Khainite, Killing Blow.

Sacred Slaughterer: Every ritual execution that Tullaris performs serves as a glorious offering to Khaine, driving the other Executioners he leads to match his skill and devotion with further slaughter. If Tullaris slays an enemy in a challenge, the Dark Elves gain a +D3 bonus to their combat resolution score, in addition to any wounds inflicted during the challenge and up to the normal overkill limit.

Tullaris the Dreaded: The Executioners unit including Tullaris causes Fear.

Magic Item
The Blade of Har Ganeth (Magic Weapon)
It is said that this weapon claimed the first victim during the great sacrifice that led to the creation of the Executioners, and that it feeds upon the blood of its decapitated victims, imbuing its wielder with magical accuracy. With it, Tullaris has slain thousands of enemies in the service of Khaine, and become a figure of dread across Naggaroth, Ulthuan and beyond.

Great weapon. The wielder may re-roll any failed rolls to wound in close combat.

THE HOST OF NAGGAROTH

The world is yours for the taking, if you have the daring and cunning to grasp it. Riches beyond avarice and a life of glory and luxury await the bold. All you need is an army of cut-throat warriors willing to obey your every command!

The Dark Elf army is a subtle weapon, like a well-placed dagger. Through guile and clever alliance, a Dark Elf general can gather a Druchii host capable of dominating on the field of battle. With the right blend of units and strategy, you will find the Dark Elf army can outmanoeuvre the foe, devastate them with magic, reap a bloody harvest with missile fire and chop apart the survivors in close combat. The hardest part may well be deciding which of these many different tactics will best suit you! Be warned, though, that you will not have an endless horde of warriors at your command, nor the brute strength of lesser races. Though your army may be a well-balanced, razor-sharp sword, you must learn to wield it with deadly accuracy.

Seize the Initiative

If you are to take what is rightfully yours, you must be bold. You should strike hard and fast and seek decisive victory. Your warriors exist to die for your glory, though this does not mean you should sacrifice them without gain. When on the attack, to ensure that you crush the enemies you face, use the manoeuvrability of your army to engage opponents with multiple units from several directions. Cold One Knights and Chariots in particular provide devastating impact and are great for making supporting charges alongside other units. Destroy one foe and then move onto the next until your enemy is utterly annihilated!

Corsairs are great for getting stuck into the enemy in this fashion. Their Sea Dragon cloaks protect them against most missile fire and with two hand weapons each they can deal out plenty of attacks. You also have some very effective fighters as your Special choices; Witch Elves, Executioners and Black Guard can all carve apart their foes in the first round of a combat. They are swifter than the majority of other infantry, and so should get the charge. Witch Elves deserve special mention. They can tear through foes such as Goblins, High Elves or Empire state troops in an instant, due to their Frenzy and Poisoned Attacks. However, use other units (Dark Riders, for instance) to ensure the Witch Elves' Frenzy doesn't cause them to charge heavily armoured foes or be led astray by skirmishers.

As you advance, be sure to protect your infantry from counter-attack by enemy cavalry or flanking units. Spearmen are ideal for this, as they are relatively cheap and can move forward with your attack whilst retaining all of the benefits of their spears if they get charged. Dark Riders are also very good at this job and are swift enough to intercept enemy flankers. Angle these protective units in such a way that if the enemy does prevail their pursuits or overruns take them away from your main regiments or into a counter-charge.

The Deadly Shadow

Within every Dark Elf unit lurks the threat of a hidden danger – Assassins! While your enemy may see where you've placed your other characters, these secret killers will always keep your opponent guessing as to what he really faces. On the attack, an Assassin can be used to kill enemy characters or simply slaughter opposing troops. On the defence, an unexpected challenge can hold up an enemy until aid arrives. Keep your Assassins hidden until the perfect moment to strike – this is not necessarily the first time the unit gets into combat. A wily foe may send in expendable troops to gauge the strength of your unit – resist the urge to reveal your Assassin until his skills will prove most decisive.

The Hail of Death

Repeater crossbows and Reaper Bolt Throwers can lay down volleys of shooting to pave the way for your attack. If combined with lots of magic, it is possible to field a stationary, defensive army that cuts down the enemy as they advance but more often your shooting should be used to soften up the enemy before your units strike. Concentrate on one or two units when possible – the big advantage of repeater crossbows is the number of shots they can fire over a small frontage. Dark Riders provide highly mobile firepower and can target enemy war machines or other hard-to-reach targets. Corsairs can also carry repeater handbows for some extra short-range shooting, backed up by their considerable close combat ability.

Spearmen are useful as guards for your war machine and missile troops. Position them in such a way that they can move forward and engage enemy units trying to get into your bolt throwers and repeater crossbows.

The Power of Sorcery

Dark Magic can be devastating, but it is also dangerous. Use the *Power of Darkness* spell freely and use your increased number of power dice to blast through your opponents dispels. As with your shooting, try as best you can to target the enemy units you are going to engage in combat to give your warriors the best chance of defeating them. Spearmen make a cheap, expendable bodyguard for a Sorceress – especially if she has the Sacrificial Dagger!

The final words of advice are simple: Hatred is your friend! Don't forget to use your re-rolls to hit!

You can find out lots more about Dark Elves army selection and tactics in White Dwarf magazine and on the Games Workshop website:

www.games-workshop.com

LORDS AND HEROES

▲ Dreadlord, mounted on Cold One.

▲ Dreadlords and Masters lead the armies of the Dark Elves.

▲ The most ornate shields are crafted for Dark Elf Dreadlords and Masters.

◄ Battle Standard bearer riding Cold One (a converted Dreadlord model).

▲ Lokhir Fellheart, ruler of the Black Ark *Tower of Blessed Dread*.

▲ Sorceress.

▲ Supreme Sorceress.

► Morathi, riding Sulaphet, the Dark Pegasus.

▲ Sorceress mounted on a Cold One.

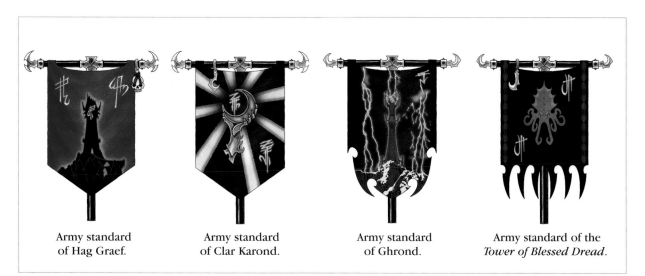

Army standard of Hag Graef.

Army standard of Clar Karond.

Army standard of Ghrond.

Army standard of the *Tower of Blessed Dread*.

DARK ELF WARRIORS

▲ Dark Elf Warriors armed with spears form the mainstay of the battleline.

Each regiment bears its own distinctive shield and banner design.

▲ Lordling.   ▲ Lordling.

Here are just a few of the many designs of Dark Elf shields.

REPEATER CROSSBOWMEN

▲ Dark Elf Repeater Crossbowmen can lay down an impressive volume of missile fire.

BLACK ARK CORSAIRS

▲ Reaver.

▲ Corsairs may swap one of their blades for a deadly handbow.

▲ Sea Dragon cloaks protect the Corsairs from enemy attacks.

COLD ONE KNIGHTS

► The fearsome Cold One Knights form a murderous shock cavalry regiment.

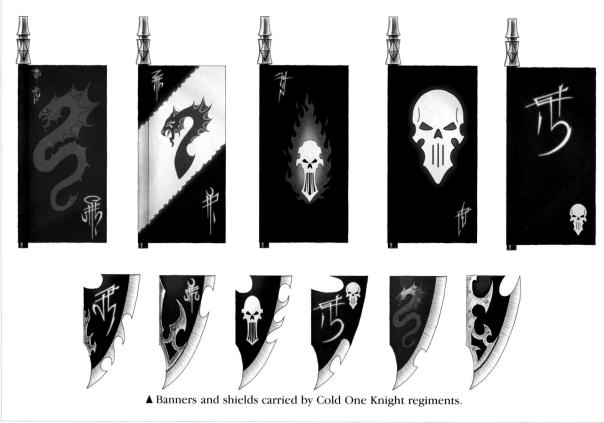

▲ Banners and shields carried by Cold One Knight regiments.

Cold Ones' scaly hides exhibit differing shades of green and may bear distinctive markings.

WITCH ELVES

▶ The Cauldron of Blood – altar to Khaine, the God of Murder.

HAR GANETH EXECUTIONERS

► Executioners go to battle bearing the lethal draich – the same deadly weapon that they use for ritual beheadings.

▲ Draich-master.

ASSASSINS

▲ Shadowblade, Master of Assassins.

BLACK GUARD OF NAGGAROND

▲ The Black Guard are the elite bodyguard of the Witch King.

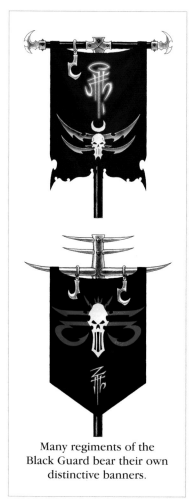

Many regiments of the Black Guard bear their own distinctive banners.

DARK RIDERS

▶ Dark Riders rove ahead of Dark Elf armies, locating enemy positions and making lightning attacks on the flanks of the opposing force.

SHADES

▲ Shades appear out of the darkness to visit death on their foes.

REAPER BOLT THROWER

Reaper Bolt Throwers can be fielded individually or in batteries of two.

MANTICORE

Dark Elf Dreadlords and Masters may choose to ride to battle atop a terrifying Manticore.

WAR HYDRA

The Host of Naggaroth

CHOOSING AN ARMY

This army list enables you to turn your Citadel miniatures collection into an army ready for tabletop battle. As described in the Warhammer rulebook, the army list is divided into four sections: Characters (including Lords and Heroes), Core Units, Special Units and Rare Units.

Choosing an Army

Every miniature in the Warhammer range has a points cost that reflects how effective it is on the battlefield. For example, a Dark Elf Warrior costs just 6 points, while a mighty Supreme Sorceress costs 225 points!

Both players choose armies to the same agreed points total. You can spend less and will probably find it impossible to use up every last point. Most '2,000 point' armies, for example, will be something like 1,998 or 1,999 points.

To form your miniatures into an army, look up the relevant army list entry for the first troop type. This tells you the points cost to add each unit of models to your army and any options or upgrades the unit may have. Then select your next unit, calculate its points and so on until you reach the agreed points total. In addition to the points, there are a few other rules that govern which units you can include in your army, as detailed under Choosing Characters and Choosing Troops.

Army List Entries

Profiles: The characteristic profiles for the model(s) in each unit are provided as a reminder. Where several profiles are required, these are also given even if they are optional.

Unit Size. Each troop entry specifies the minimum size for each unit, which is the smallest number of models needed to form that unit. In some cases units also have a maximum size.

Equipment. Each entry lists the standard weapons and armour for that unit type. The cost of these items is included in the basic points value. Additional or optional weapons and armour cost extra and are covered in the Options section of the unit entry.

Options. Many entries list different weapon, armour and equipment options, along with any additional points cost for giving them to the unit. This includes magic items and other upgrades for characters. It may also include the option to upgrade a unit member to a musician, champion, or standard bearer. Where units are given options for weapons, the entire unit must be equipped the same.

Special Rules. Many troops have special rules that are fully described earlier in this book. The names of these rules are listed as a reminder.

Choosing Characters

Characters are divided into two categories: **Lords** and **Heroes.** The maximum number of characters an army can include is shown on the chart below. Of these, only a certain number can be Lords. A character mounted on a Black Dragon or a Master on a Manticore takes up an extra 'Hero' choice.

Army Points Value	Total Characters	Max. Lords
Less than 2,000	3	0
2,000 or more	4	1
3,000 or more	6	2
4,000 or more	8	3
Each +1,000	+2	+1

A army must always include at least one character to act as its **General**. If you include more than one character, then the one with the highest Leadership value is the general. When one or more characters have the same (and highest) Leadership, choose one to be the General at the start of the battle. Make sure that your opponent knows which character is your General when you deploy your army.

Many characters can be equipped with magic items, representing ancient weapons, and other artefacts of considerable age and potency. Where characters have this option, it is included in their individual entries.

Choosing Troops

The number of each type of unit allowed depends on the army's points value.

For **Core** units, there is a minimum number of units from this category that you must take. Harpies do not count towards this minimum number of Core units.

For **Special** and **Rare** units, there is a maximum number of units that you can field.

Army Points Value	Core Units	Special Units	Rare Units
Less than 2,000	2+	0-3	0-1
2,000 or more	3+	0-4	0-2
3,000 or more	4+	0-5	0-3
4,000 or more	5+	0-6	0-4
Each +1,000	+ 1 minimum	+0-1	+0-1

Like many characters, some units can be equipped with magic items (normally a banner). Where units have this option, it is included in their individual entries.

LORDS

Malekith, the Witch King　600 Points

Page 64

	M	WS	BS	S	T	W	I	A	LD
Malekith	5	8	6	5	4	3	8	4	10

You may only include one Malekith in your army

Magic:
- Malekith is a Level 4 Wizard and knows spells from the Lore of Dark Magic.

Equipment:
- Destroyer
- Armour of Midnight
- Spellshield
- Circlet of Iron

Special Rules:
- Eternal Hatred
- Absolute Power
- Immune to Psychology

Options:

Mount (one choice only):

Cold One	**30pts**
Black Dragon	**320pts**
The Black Chariot (with one other crewman)	**110pts**

Morathi, the Hag Sorceress　455 Points

Page 65

	M	WS	BS	S	T	W	I	A	LD
Morathi	5	5	4	3	3	3	6	3	10
Sulephet	8	4	0	4	4	3	4	3	6

You may only include one Morathi in your army

Magic:
- Morathi is a Level 4 Wizard and knows all of the spells from the Lore of Dark Magic.

Equipment:
- Hand weapon

Mount:
- Morathi rides the Dark Pegasus, Sulephet.

Special Rules:
- Eternal Hatred
- Druchii Sorcery
- Thousand and One Dark Blessings
- Enchanting Beauty
- The First Sorceress

Options:

Magic Weapon (must take one choice only):

Heartrender	**45pts**
Darksword	**25pts**

Magic Items:
May take any one Arcane Item and/or one Enchanted Item for the points costs listed on pages 100 and 103.

Crone Hellebron, The Hag Queen　350 Points

Page 66

	M	WS	BS	S	T	W	I	A	LD
Hellebron	5	7	6	4	3	3	9	4	10

You may only include one Hellebron in your army

Queen of Khaine: When Hellebron is your General, Witch Elves are Core Units.

Equipment:
- Deathsword
- Parrying Blade
- Amulet of Fire

Special Rules:
- Eternal Hatred
- Khainite
- Frenzy
- Two Magic Weapons
- Queen of Khaine

Options:

Mount (one choice only):

Manticore	**200pts**

Gifts of Khaine (see page 99):
- Rune of Khaine
- Witchbrew
- Cry of War

LORDS

Dreadlord 140 Points

Page 60

	M	WS	BS	S	T	W	I	A	LD
Dreadlord	5	7	6	4	3	3	8	4	10

Equipment: Hand weapon.

Special Rules:
- Eternal Hatred

Options:

Close Combat Weapon (one choice only):
Lance **6pts**
Great Weapon **6pts**
Halberd **6pts**
Additional hand weapon **6pts**

Ranged Weapon (one choice only):
Repeater Crossbow **10pts**
Repeater handbow **8pts**
Pair of repeater handbows **16pts**
Armour:
Light armour* **3pts**
Heavy armour* **6pts**
 *May not choose both
Shield **3pts**
Sea Dragon Cloak **6pts**

Mount (one choice only):
Dark Steed **18pts**
Cold One **30pts**
Dark Pegasus **50pts**
Manticore **200pts**
Black Dragon **320pts**
Cold One chariot (replacing one crew) **90pts**

Magic Items:
Up to a total of **100pts**

Supreme Sorceress 225 Points

Page 62

	M	WS	BS	S	T	W	I	A	LD
Supreme Sorceress	5	4	4	3	3	3	5	1	9

Magic:
- A Supreme Sorceress is a Level 3 Wizard and knows spells from one of the following Lores: Dark Magic, Fire, Shadow, Metal or Death.

Equipment:
- Hand weapon

Special Rules:
- Eternal Hatred
- Druchii Sorcery

Options:

Magic:
Upgrade to Level 4 Wizard **35pts**

Mount (one choice only):
Dark Steed **18pts**
Cold One **30pts**
Dark Pegasus **50pts**
Manticore **200pts**
Black Dragon **320pts**

Magic Items:
Up to a total of **100pts**

Character Mounts

	M	WS	BS	S	T	W	I	A	LD
Dark Steed	9	3	0	3	3	1	4	1	5
Cold One	7	3	0	4	4	1	2	1	3
Dark Pegasus	8	3	0	4	4	3	4	2	6
Manticore	6	5	0	5	5	4	5	4	5
Black Dragon	6	6	0	6	6	3	5	8

Special Rules:
- Cold One (p55): Stupidity, Fear, Thick-skinned
- Dark Pegasus (p56): Fly, Impale Attack
- Manticore (p59): Fly, Terror, Large Target, Killing Blow, Uncontrollable
- Black Dragon (p57): Fly, Terror, Large Target, 3+ Scaly Skin, Noxious Breath.

A model mounted on a Black Dragon (including Malekith) or a Master (but not a Dreadlord) mounted on a Manticore takes up one additional Hero 'choice' you are allowed to make.

HEROES

Malus Darkblade, Scion of Hag Graef　275 Points

Page 67

	M	WS	BS	S	T	W	I	A	LD
Malus	5	6	5	4	3	2	7	3	9
Spite	7	3	0	4	4	1	2	2	4

You may only include one Malus in your army

Equipment:
- Heavy armour
- Warpsword of Khaine

Mount:
- Malus rides the Cold One, Spite.

Special Rules:
- Eternal Hatred
- Tz'arkan
- Not Just a Dumb Brute

Shadowblade, Master of Assassins　300 Points

Page 68

	M	WS	BS	S	T	W	I	A	LD
Shadowblade	6	10	10	4	3	2	10	3	10

You may only include one Shadowblade in your army

Equipment:
- Two hand weapons
- Heart of Woe
- Potion of Strength

Special Rules:
- Eternal Hatred
- Khainite
- Poisoned Attacks
- Master of Assassins
- Always Strikes First
- Scout
- A Killer not a Leader

Gifts of Khaine
(see page 99):
- Rending Stars
- Dance of Doom
- Touch of Death
- Hand of Khaine
- Dark Venom

Lokhir Fellheart, Captain of the Tower of Blessed Dread　250 Points

Page 69

	M	WS	BS	S	T	W	I	A	LD
Lokhir	5	6	6	4	3	2	7	3	9

You may only include one Lokhir in your army

Equipment:
- The Red Blades
- Sea Dragon Cloak
- Helm of the Kraken

Special Rules:
- Eternal Hatred
- Merciless Slaver
- Daring Leap

Sorceress　100 Points

Page 62

	M	WS	BS	S	T	W	I	A	LD
Sorceress	5	4	4	3	3	2	5	1	8

Equipment:
- Hand weapon

Special Rules:
- Eternal Hatred
- Druchii Sorcery

Magic:
A Sorceress is a Level 1 Wizard and knows spells from one of the following Lores: Dark Magic, Fire, Metal, Shadow, or Death.

Options:

Magic:
Upgrade to Level 2 Wizard **35pts**

Mount (one choice only):
Dark Steed **12pts**
Cold One **20pts**
Dark Pegasus **50pts**

Magic Items:
Up to a total of **50pts**

HEROES

Master* 80 Points

Page 60

	M	WS	BS	S	T	W	I	A	LD
Master	5	6	6	4	3	2	7	3	9

Equipment:
- Hand weapon

Special Rules:
- Eternal Hatred

Options:

Close Combat Weapon (one choice only):

Lance **4pts**
Great weapon **4pts**
Halberd **4pts**
Additional hand weapon **4pts**
Beastmaster's scourge **6pts**

Ranged Weapon (one choice only):

Repeater crossbow **10pts**
Repeater handbow **8pts**
Pair of repeater handbows **16pts**

Armour:
Light armour* **2pts**
Heavy armour* **4pts**
  *May not choose both
Shield **2pts**
Sea Dragon Cloak **4pts**

Mount (one choice only):
Dark Steed **12pts**
Cold One **20pts**
Dark Pegasus **50pts**
Manticore **200pts**
Cold One chariot (replacing one crew) **90pts**

Magic Items:
Up to a total of **50pts**

Death Hag* 90 Points

Page 50

	M	WS	BS	S	T	W	I	A	LD
Death Hag	5	6	6	4	3	2	8	3	9

Equipment:
- Two hand weapons

Special Rules:
- Eternal Hatred
- Frenzy
- Khainite
- Poisoned Attacks

Options:

Upgrades:
Cauldron of Blood **110pts**

Gifts of Khaine:
Up to a total of **50pts**

CAULDRON OF BLOOD

	M	WS	BS	S	T	W	I	A	LD
Hag	5	4	4	3	3	1	6	2	8

Unit size: 2 Hags and 1 Cauldron of Blood.

Equipment: Two hand weapons.

Special Rules:
- Eternal Hatred, Frenzy, Khainite, War Machine, Terror, Magic Resistance (1), Attendants, Blessings of Khaine, Altar of Khaine, Poisoned Attacks.

If a Death Hag chooses a Cauldron of Blood, she becomes part of the unit and cannot leave it during the battle.

---

*BATTLE STANDARD BEARER

One Master or Death Hag in the army may carry the Battle Standard for +25 points. If a Hero is carrying the Battle Standard, he can have a magic banner (no points limit), but if he carries a magic banner he cannot carry any other magic items. A Death Hag may have Gifts of Khaine as normal (except those that are also magic items).

CORE

Dark Elf Warriors 6 Points per model

Page 44

	M	WS	BS	S	T	W	I	A	LD
Dark Elf Warrior	5	4	4	3	3	1	5	1	8
Lordling	5	4	4	3	3	1	5	2	8

Unit size:
10+

Equipment:
- Hand weapon
- Spear
- Light armour

Special Rules:
- Eternal Hatred

Options:

Command:
Upgrade one Dark Elf to a Lordling **6pts**
Upgrade one Dark Elf to a Musician **3pts**
Upgrade one Dark Elf to a Standard Bearer **6pts**
  May carry a magic standard worth up to **25pts**

Armour:
Shield .... **1pt per model**

Dark Elf Repeater Crossbowmen 10 Points per model

Page 44

	M	WS	BS	S	T	W	I	A	LD
Dark Elf Crossbowman	5	4	4	3	3	1	5	1	8
Guardmaster	5	4	5	3	3	1	5	1	8

Unit size:
10+

Equipment:
- Hand weapon
- Repeater crossbow
- Light armour

Special Rules:
- Eternal Hatred

Options:

Command:
Upgrade one Dark Elf to a Guardmaster **5pts**
Upgrade one Dark Elf to a Musician **5pts**
Upgrade one Dark Elf to a Standard Bearer **10pts**

Armour:
Shield .... **1pt per model**

Black Ark Corsairs 10 Points per model

Page 45

	M	WS	BS	S	T	W	I	A	LD
Corsair	5	4	4	3	3	1	5	1	8
Reaver	5	4	4	3	3	1	5	2	8

Unit size:
10+

Equipment:
- Two hand weapons
- Light armour
- Sea Dragon cloak

Special Rules:
- Eternal Hatred
- Slavers

Options:

Command:
Upgrade one Corsair to a Reaver **10pts**
Upgrade one Corsair to a Musician **5pts**
Upgrade one Corsair to a Standard Bearer **10pts**
  May carry a magic standard worth up to **25pts**

Weapons:
Swap hand weapon for handbow .... **free**
Give pair of handbows to Reaver **3pts**

CORE

Dark Riders 17 Points per model

Page 49

	M	WS	BS	S	T	W	I	A	LD
Dark Rider	5	4	4	3	3	1	5	1	8
Herald	5	4	5	3	3	1	5	2	8
Dark Steed	9	3	0	3	3	1	4	1	5

Unit size:
5+

Equipment:
• Hand weapon
• Spear
• Light armour

Special Rules:
• Eternal Hatred
• Fast Cavalry
  (unless
  equipped with
  shields)

Options:

Command:
Upgrade one Dark Rider to a Herald **14pts**
Upgrade one Dark Rider to a Musician **7pts**
Upgrade one Dark Rider to a Standard Bearer **14pts**

Armour:
Shield ....**1pt per model**

Weapons:
Repeater Crossbows ....**5pts per model**

Harpies 11 Points per model

Page 55

	M	WS	BS	S	T	W	I	A	LD
Harpy	5	3	0	3	3	1	5	2	6

Harpies do not count towards the minimum number of
Core units you must include in your army.

Unit size: 5-10

Equipment:
• Vicious claws and
  temperament
  (hand weapon)

Special Rules:
• Flying Unit
• Beasts

Dark Elf Assassin 90 Points

Page 61

	M	WS	BS	S	T	W	I	A	LD
Assassin	5	9	9	4	3	2	10	3	10

Each Dark Elf infantry unit (except Harpies) may
include a single Assassin. See the Hidden rule for
details. Assassins are characters but do not fill any
character or Core selections in your army

Equipment:
• Hand weapon

Special Rules:
• Eternal Hatred
• Khainite
• Scout
• Poisoned Attacks
  (hand weapons and
  handbow)
• Always Strikes First
• Hidden
• A Killer not a Leader

Options:

Weapons:
Additional hand weapon **6pts**
Repeater handbow **10pts**

Gifts of Khaine:
Up to a total of **75pts**

SPECIAL

Witch Elves   10 Points per model

	M	WS	BS	S	T	W	I	A	LD
Witch Elf	5	4	4	3	3	1	6	1	8
Hag	5	4	4	3	3	1	6	2	8

Unit size:
5+

Equipment:
• Two hand weapons

Special Rules:
• Eternal Hatred
• Frenzy
• Khainite
• Poisoned Attacks

Options:

Command:
Upgrade one Witch Elf to a Hag **10pts**
Upgrade one Witch Elf to a Musician **5pts**
Upgrade one Witch Elf to a Standard Bearer **10pts**
    May carry a magic standard worth up to **25pts**

Gifts of Khaine (Hag only):
Up to a total of **25pts**

Shades   16 Points per model

Page 48

	M	WS	BS	S	T	W	I	A	LD
Shade	5	5	5	3	3	1	5	1	8
Bloodshade	5	5	6	3	3	1	5	2	8

Unit size:
5+

Equipment:
• Hand weapon
• Repeater crossbow

Special Rules:
• Eternal Hatred
• Skirmishers
• Scouts

Options:

Command:
Upgrade one Shade to a Bloodshade **18pts**

Weapons (one choice only)
Great weapon ....**2pts per model**
Additional hand weapon ....**1pt per model**

Armour:
Light armour ....**1 pts per model**

Har Ganeth Executioners   12 Points per model

Page 47

	M	WS	BS	S	T	W	I	A	LD
Executioner	5	5	4	4	3	1	5	1	8
Draich-master	5	5	4	4	3	1	5	2	8

Unit size:
5+

Equipment:
• Great weapon
• Hand weapon
• Heavy armour

Special Rules:
• Eternal Hatred
• Khainite
• Killing Blow

Options:

Command:
Upgrade one Executioner to a Draich-master **12pts**
Upgrade one Executioner to a Musician **6pts**
Upgrade one Executioner to a Standard Bearer **12pts**
    May carry a magic standard worth up to **25pts**
One Executioner unit in the army may include Tullaris
    of Har Ganeth instead of a Draich-master **95pts**

Tullaris of Har Ganeth

Page 71

	M	WS	BS	S	T	W	I	A	LD
Tullaris	5	5	4	4	3	1	5	2	8

Tullaris is a Champion in all regards.

Equipment:
• The Blade of Har Ganeth
• Heavy armour

Special Rules:
• Eternal Hatred
• Khainite
• Killing Blow
• Sacred Slaughterer
• Tullaris the Dreaded

SPECIAL

Cold One Knights   27 Points per model

Page 52

	M	WS	BS	S	T	W	I	A	LD
Cold One Knight	5	5	4	4	3	1	6	1	9
Dread Knight	5	5	4	4	3	1	6	2	9
Cold One	7	3	0	4	4	1	2	1	3

Unit size:
5+

Mount:
• Cold One

Equipment:
• Hand weapon
• Heavy armour
• Lance
• Shield

Special Rules:
• Eternal Hatred
• Stupidity
• Fear
• Thick-skinned

Options:

Command:
Upgrade one Knight to a Dread Knight **16pts**
Upgrade one Knight to a Musician **8pts**
Upgrade one Knight to a Standard Bearer **16pts**
   May carry a magic standard worth up to **50pts**

Magic Items (Dread Knight only):
Up to a total of **25pts**

Cold One Chariot   100 Points

Page 53

	M	WS	BS	S	T	W	I	A	LD
Chariot	-	-	-	5	5	4	-	-	-
Charioteer	-	5	4	4	-	-	6	1	9
Cold One	7	3	0	4	-	-	2	1	-

Unit size: 1 scythed chariot ridden by 2 charioteers and drawn by 2 Cold Ones.

Armour saving throw: 3+.

Equipment:
Crew have:
• Spears
• Hand weapons
• Repeater Crossbows

Special Rules:
• Eternal Hatred
• Stupidity
• Chariot
• Cause Fear

Black Guard of Naggarond   13 Points per model

Page 46

	M	WS	BS	S	T	W	I	A	LD
Black Guard	5	5	4	3	3	1	6	2	9
Tower Master	5	5	4	3	3	1	6	3	9

Unit size:
5-20

Equipment:
• Hand weapon
• Heavy armour
• Halberd

Special Rules:
• Eternal Hatred
• Immune to Psychology
• Warrior Elite
• Stubborn

Options:

Command:
Upgrade one Black Guard to a Tower Master **14pts**
Upgrade one Black Guard to a Musician **7pts**
Upgrade one Black Guard to a Standard Bearer ...**14pts**
   May carry a magic standard worth up to **50pts**
One Black Guard unit in the army may include Kouran
   instead of a Tower Master **75pts**

Magic Items (Tower Master only):
Up to a total of **25pts**

Kouran of the Black Guard

Page 70

	M	WS	BS	S	T	W	I	A	LD
Kouran	5	5	4	3	3	1	6	3	9

Kouran is a Champion in all regards.

Equipment:
• The Crimson Death
• The Armour of Grief

Special Rules:
• Eternal Hatred
• Warrior Elite
• Captain of the Black Guard

RARE

Reaper Bolt Thrower 100 Points

Page 54

	M	WS	BS	S	T	W	I	A	LD
Dark Elf	5	4	4	3	3	1	5	1	8
Reaper	-	-	-	-	7	3	-	-	-

You may include 1 or 2 Reaper Bolt Throwers as a single Rare choice. These are separate units.

Unit size: 1 Reaper Bolt Thrower with 2 crew.

Equipment:
- Hand weapon
- Light armour

Special Rules:
- Eternal Hatred
- War Machine

War Hydra 175 Points

Page 58

	M	WS	BS	S	T	W	I	A	LD
War Hydra	6	4	0	5	5	5	2	7	6
Beastmaster	6	4	4	3	3	1	5	2	8

Unit size: 1 War Hydra with 2 Beastmasters.

Equipment:
- The Beastmasters are each armed with a Beastmaster's scourge and a hand weapon.

Special Rules (Hydra):
- Eternal Hatred
- 4+ Scaly Skin
- Large Target
- Terror
- Fiery Breath
- Regenerate
- Monster and Handlers

(Beastmasters):
- Eternal Hatred
- Beastmasters

GIFTS OF KHAINE

The Assassins and Witch Elves of Khaine have access to many exotic weapons, poisons, abilities and unique artefacts. These Gifts of Khaine may be taken by certain models as indicated in the army list. Unless otherwise stated, these are not magic items. A model may not have multiples of the same upgrade, but an upgrade can be taken by more than one model in the army.

Rending Stars (Assassins only)   **30 points**
These are a particular type of throwing star, with wickedly curved edges that tear through flesh and leave a deeply lacerated wound.
Maximum Range: 12"; **Strength:** As user+1.
Rules: Thrown weapon; multiple shot x3.

Dance of Doom   **30 points**
The sinuous Dance of Doom can be used to dodge the fastest shot or blow.
The model has a 5+ ward save.

Touch of Death   **30 points**
The Adepts of Death school the servants of Khaine to learn the points on a body that kill instantly.
The model has killing blow.

Rune of Khaine   **25 points**
The Hag Queens burn the rune of the Lord of Murder upon the brow of the most zealous of killers.
The model has +D3 Attacks (rolled just before making the model's attacks).

Witchbrew (Hags only)   **25 points**
Witchbrew is distilled from blood by the Hag Queens. It drives Witch Elves into such an ecstasy of destruction that they will fight on against impossible odds.
Witchbrew affects the Hag's unit for the entire battle. Enemy units cannot claim combat resolution bonuses for outnumbering, flank or rear attacks, or higher ground if they are only fighting a unit affected by Witchbrew.

MAGIC ITEMS
These two Gifts of Khaine follow all of the normal rules for magic items (e.g. only one per army, etc.).

Venom Sword (Magic weapon)   **75 points**
The Venom Sword is quenched in the poison of a thousand malicious serpents. When it strikes, mystical poisons flow into the veins of its victim.
Magic weapon. Any model that takes a wound from the Venom Sword (after saves, etc) must roll equal to or under its Toughness on 2D6 or automatically lose all remaining wounds.

Cloak of Twilight (Enchanted item)   **20 points**
Assassin only
Bound spell, power level 3.
Imbued with the darkness of a moonless night, this cloak allows the wearer to move rapidly and unseen.
The Cloak of Twilight contains the *Steed of Shadows* spell from the Lore of Shadows.

Hand of Khaine   **15 points**
Tracing a complex pattern in the air, the Dark Elf entrances his victim, leaving him vulnerable and open to attack.
One model in base contact chosen by the Dark Elves player, or the model's opponent in a challenge, loses one Attack (to a minimum of 1). Against mounted models, the Dark Elves player must choose either the mount or the rider. If the model has special types of attack (a Giant, for example) the Hand of Khaine has no effect. Models that are Immune to Psychology are unaffected by the Hand of Khaine.

Cry of War   **10 points**
By screeching one of the seventeen secret names of Khaine, the warrior freezes enemies with horror.
A unit charged by a warrior with a Cry of War must pass a Leadership test or reduce their Weapon Skill by 1 (to a minimum of 1) for that Close Combat.

TOXINS

All of a model's non-magic weapons may be coated with one type of toxin (replacing its Poisoned Attacks). These toxins have no additional effect against models that are immune to Poisoned Attacks.

Manbane   **25 points**
Manbane is one of the most lethal venoms ever devised, causing even the tiniest wound to bleed openly and profusely.
A model with a weapon coated with Manbane always counts their Strength as one higher than their target's Toughness, unless their Strength would normally be more than this, up to a maximum of Strength 6. This means that they almost always wound opponents on a roll of 3+. This modified Strength is used to calculate armour save modifiers.

Black Lotus   **20 points**
Black Lotus has a terrifying effect on living flesh, driving victims delusional and insane.
The model may re-roll any dice that score a 1 when rolling to wound with a weapon coated with Black Lotus.

Dark Venom   **10 points**
A weapon treated with Dark Venom will cause a mortal wound if it merely scratches the skin, causing the poisoned victim to die in the most grotesque manner imaginable.
If a model with Dark Venom slays an enemy in a challenge, all wounds inflicted by the model in the challenge that round are doubled for the purposes of combat resolution scores (up to the overkill maximum).

TREASURES OF NAGGAROTH

In this section, the Common magic items are listed first (see the Warhammer rulebook for a complete description). These are followed by a list of 'Dark Elves only' magic items. These items can only be used by models from this book. Magic items must be selected within the points limitations set by the army list section. Note that the rules for magic items presented in the Warhammer rulebook also apply to the 'Dark Elves only' magic items.

COMMON MAGIC ITEMS

Sword of Striking ....15 points
Weapon; +1 to hit

Sword of Battle ....15 points
Weapon; +1 Attack

Sword of Might ....15 points
Weapon; +1 Strength

Biting Blade ....5 points
Weapon; -1 armour save

Enchanted Shield ....15 points
Armour; 5+ armour save

Talisman of Protection ....15 points
Talisman; 6+ ward save

Staff of Sorcery ....35 points
Arcane; +1 to dispel

Dispel Scroll ....25 points
Arcane; one use only; Automatically dispel an enemy spell.

Power Stone ....20 points
Arcane; one use only; +2 dice to cast a spell.

War Banner ....25 points
Banner; +1 combat resolution

ENCHANTED ITEMS

Deathmask   50 points
Made from enchanted gold of the Blackspine Mountains, the Deathmask depicts Khaine in his aspect of the Deathbringer, the merciless slayer.

The character causes terror.

The Hydra's Teeth   40 points
Taken from the corpse of a slain War Hydra, each of these fangs is finely sculpted into a skeletal figurine. They are enchanted with dark magic to summon forth those slain by the Hydra while it was alive.

The model has five Hydra's Teeth. Each can be used once as a thrown weapon with a range of 12". Declare how many of its Hydra's Teeth the model is throwing before rolling to hit – there is no 'multiple shots' penalty for throwing more than one tooth at a time. For each hit, make D6 WS2 S3 close combat attacks against the target unit. Up to two attacks per turn can be allocated by the Dark Elves player against each character or Champion in the unit.

Crystal of Midnight   35 points
Inside this black glowing crystal is a malignant captured spirit, which can be unleashed to seek out the mind of an enemy magic user and steal their thoughts.

One use only. Nominate another Wizard anywhere on the table at the start of any Dark Elves turn. The Wizard must pass a Leadership test on 3D6 otherwise they forget one randomly determined spell for the rest of the battle.

Black Dragon Egg   30 points
Many of the eggs laid by Malekith's Black Dragons do not develop into full hatchlings. When eaten, the properties of the Dragon are temporarily passed on.

One use only. The model may consume the Black Dragon Egg at the start of any player turn. For the remainder of that turn the model has Toughness 6 and the Noxious Breath attack (see page 61).

Potion of Strength   30 points
A potent magical brew created from Troll blood and the heart of a Griffon.

One use only. The model may drink this at the start of any close combat and it lasts until the start of the next player's turn. While it is in effect, the Potion of Strength grants +3 Strength.

Gem of Nightmares   25 points
When the magic of this dark stone is unleashed, the bearer is surrounded by a vortex of whirling, wailing apparitions that burn with dark flames.

One use only. The Gem of Nightmares can be used at the start of any turn. Until the end of that turn, the model and any unit it has joined cause Fear.

The Guiding Eye   25 points
Wrought in black iron with a oval ruby at its centre, the Guiding Eye grants mystical sight to the wearer.

One use only. The character and any unit he joins may re-roll missed shooting to hit rolls.

MAGIC WEAPONS

Executioner's Axe (Models on foot only)   80 points
The Executioner's Axe is a huge, black-bladed weapon bound with spells of dismemberment. A single blow from it can cut any opponent in half.

Requires two hands. Strikes last. In close combat, the wielder counts as having a Strength double that of their target's Toughness, up to a maximum of Strength 10. In addition, the Executioner's Axe causes D3 wounds.

Sword of Ruin   50 points
This magical sword can cleave through armour as if it were air.

No armour saves may be taken against hits from the Sword of Ruin.

Web of Shadows   50 points
Woven from the hair of Witch Elves and studded with ensorcelled Harpy fangs, a victim caught in the Web of Shadows will be ripped to shreds.

One use only. The character uses the Web of Shadows instead of making any normal attacks that round. When used, one model in base contact with the character automatically takes 2D6 Strength 3 hits. Wounds caused do not carry over on to other models. A model with the Web of Shadows may instead choose to use a mundane weapon in any round of combat.

Chillblade   50 points
This sword holds a terrible spell of coldness that seeps into the Dark Elf's victim, freezing their soul and temporarily paralysing them.

Enemy models suffering hits from the Chillblade must pass a Toughness test for every hit. If a test is failed the model suffers a wound with no armour save. Models suffering a wound (after ward saves, etc) may not make any close combat attacks that turn. No normal roll to wound is made for attacks with the Chillblade.

Heartseeker   35 points
Heartseeker has an uncanny ability to find the heart of a living thing. Dark Elves delight in its ability to destroy the lifeforce of their victims.

The character may re-roll all failed rolls to hit and to wound in close combat.

Hydra Blade   35 points
The Hydra Blade strikes repeatedly, like its many-headed namesake.

A character wielding the Hydra Blade gains D3 additional attacks (roll just before making attacks).

Caledor's Bane   35 points
This dire lance is etched with the fiery blood of Dragons and is much feared by High Elf Princes from the realm of Caledor.

+3 Strength on the charge. Models may not use Scaly Skin saving throws against hits from Caledor's Bane.

Dagger of Hotek   30 points
Created by Hotek, a renegade priest of Vaul, this blade allows the wielder to strike with blinding speed.

The Dagger of Hotek is an additional hand weapon, (it can be used with a mundane hand weapon) and grants the bearer the Always Strikes First special rule.

Lifetaker   30 points
Lifetaker is a repeater crossbow fashioned from blackest steel, with bolts dipped in the venom of a Black Dragon.

Range: 30"   **Str:** 4   **Rules:** Multiple Shot x3
Lifetaker always hits on a roll of 2+, regardless of any to hit modifiers, magic items, etc.

Crimson Death   25 points
This huge halberd was carried to battle by Dark Lord Khalak of Ghrond, the first Captain of the Black Guard. It has been passed down to every Captain to have succeeded him.

Requires two hands to use. A model wielding Crimson Death always strikes with Strength 6. No other modifiers or magic items can ever modify this.

Deathpiercer   25 points
This lance is tipped with a blade carved from the claws of two dozen Cold Ones. It leaves ragged wounds that see its victims swiftly bleed to death.

Lance. Killing blow.

Whip of Agony   25 points
Belonging to the feared Beastlord Rakarth, the Whip of Agony inflicts pain that even the most thick-skinned and mindless creature can feel.

Beastmaster's scourge. A model wielding the Whip of Agony always strikes with Strength 5. No other modifiers or magic items can ever modify this.

Soulrender   15 points
When it was forged, this long blade was quenched in a Cauldron of Blood and can slice through steel as easily as bone.

Great weapon. Armour piercing.

MAGIC ARMOUR

Armour of Living Death   60 points
It is claimed that anyone wearing this armour cannot die, sustained by its magical energy. Unfortunately, they cannot remove the armour and are driven insane by its magic.

Heavy armour. In addition, the model has +1 Toughness and +1 Wound. Roll a D6 before deploying any models. On a roll of a 1, the wearer succumbs to the Armour of Living Death and is subject to stupidity for the battle.

Armour of Eternal Servitude   35 points
Oaths of loyalty and dedication to Khaine were sworn at the time of the armour's forging, and the wearer is granted extended life to serve their god.

Heavy armour. The wearer can Regenerate.

Cloak of Hag Graef   25 points
Made from the scales of Aggraunir, the first sea dragon to be captured by the Dark Elves, the Cloak of Hag Graef can withstand the harshest of blows.

Sea Dragon cloak. In addition, any ranged attack hits on the character (including shooting, magic missiles and other spells with a Strength value) have their Strength halved before rolling to wound (rounding up).

Armour of Darkness   25 points
Forged from black meteoric steel, this suit is almost impossible to pierce.

This armour gives a total save of 1+ that cannot be further increased in any way (with a shield, chariot, mount and so on).

Shield of Ghrond   25 points
Shaped into the leering face of an Ice Daemon, the shield of Ghrond is imbued with the power of the magical North wind, which robs attacks of their force.

The Shield of Ghrond is treated like a normal shield, and in addition all hits the character suffers will be resolved with -1 Strength.

Blood Armour   15 points
When anointed with the blood of the foe, this armour becomes ever more endurable.

Heavy armour. For every unsaved wound the wearer inflicts in close combat, this save is improved by one point (to 4+ then 3+, etc) to a maximum total of 1+ (including any other bonuses for a shield, Sea Dragon cloak, and so on).

TALISMANS

Black Amulet   70 points
Cast from the heartstone of a mountain tainted with the power of Dark Sorcery, the Black Amulet is a lustrous polished stone of midnight hue, engraved with a single glowing rune.

The wearer has a 4+ ward save. If the wearer of the Black Amulet passes their ward save in close combat, then the attacking model suffers 1 wound instead (with no armour save allowed).

Ring of Darkness   40 points
Billowing black smoke emerges from the opal set into this ring, clouding the wearer's position.

All close combat attacks directed against the model are at half WS. Any shooting at the character or their unit is at half BS. Round fractions up.

Pendant of Khaeleth   35 points
Worn by the first High Mistress of the Dark Convent, this amulet's protective aura grows greater the stronger the blow landed upon it.

This gives a ward save, based upon the Strength of the hit. Roll a D6 for every wound suffered by the wearer, on a roll equal to or under the attack's Strength, the hit is ignored. Rolls of 6 always fail.

Seal of Ghrond   30 points
This iron seal is blessed by the priestesses of Khaine to ward away hated magic.

Add 1 dice to the dispel dice pool.

Pearl of Infinite Bleakness   25 points
Swirled with red and black veins, this magical pearl emits an aura of soul-numbing depression.

The character and his unit are Immune to Psychology.

Ring of Hotek   25 points
Hotek the renegade priest of Vaul made this ring to protect himself from the magical forces used in the forging of his artefacts.

Any Wizard (friend or foe) attempting to cast or target a spell within 12" of the wearer will suffer a Miscast on the roll of any double.

Null Talisman   15 points
These silver pendants ward away the energy of Chaos.

The Null Talisman grants magic resistance (1). Models may carry multiple Null Talismans, just like scrolls, and their effects are cumulative. For example, two Talismans confer magic resistance (2).

ARCANE ITEMS

Black Staff   **55 points**
A Black Staff is the much-desired talisman of one of the six High Mistresses of the Convent of Sorceresses.

Bound Spell, Power Level 4. Contains the Power of Darkness spell (page 63)

Focus Familiar   **25 points**
An impish familiar accompanies the Sorceress, through which she can direct her powers. This allows her to target enemies further away and out of sight.

The Focus Familiar allows the wielder to cast spells from a different position on the battlefield. Place a marker at the start of each Dark Elf Magic phase within 6" of the Sorceress and at least 1" away from enemies. She may use this position when determining range and line of sight for her spells, and whether she counts as in combat or not.

Darkstar Cloak   **25 points**
Woven into the fabric of this cloak is the essence of a star stolen from the night sky of Nagarythe.

The cloak gives the Sorceress +1 power dice in each Magic phase. Only she may use this extra dice.

Sacrificial Dagger   **25 points**
Bound with enchantments of bloodletting and spirit-binding, the sacrificial dagger is used to leech the life force from its victims and channel it into raw magic.

Once per spell-casting attempt, after the casting dice have been rolled, the Sorceress may sacrifice a model in a unit she has joined – the model is removed immediately. The Sorceress gains a power dice that must be rolled and added to the casting total (before dispel attempts). Note that it is possible for the unit to require a panic test if she sacrifices 25+% of the unit in a single Magic Phase!

Tome of Furion   **15 points**
The Dark Elf Furion of Clar Karond inscribed this book onto sheets of flayed Orcskin to teach the Path of Darkness to the uninitiated.

The Tome of Furion grants its bearer 1 additional spell.

MAGIC STANDARDS

Banner of Nagarythe   **125 points**
The Banner of Nagarythe, the standard of Northern Ulthuan that now lies beneath the ocean, is the personal banner of the Witch King, proclaiming his reign over the Elven Kingdoms.

This standard gives an additional +1 to the combat resolution score of friendly units in combat within 12", and the unit containing the banner is Unbreakable.

Hydra Banner   **75 points**
Imbued with the magic of Hekarti the Hydra Queen, this banner quickens the reflexes so that those nearby strike with her own speed and savagery.

All models in the unit gain +1 Attack in the first round of any hand-to-hand combat (including mounts).

Dread Banner   **40 points**
Such is the supernatural fear instilled by the visage of the Bloody Handed God upon this standard that few dare to even look at it.

The unit carrying this standard causes Fear.

Standard of Slaughter   **35 points**
Anointed with the blood of an Ulthuan Elf, this banner imbues its regiment with a bitter determination.

On any turn the unit with the Standard of Slaughter charges, the banner adds +D3 to the unit's combat resolution.

Standard of Hag Graef   **35 points**
Under the mystical influence of this serpentine banner, warriors strike with astounding speed.

All models in the unit containing the Standard of Hag Graef gain the Always Strikes First rule.

Sea Serpent Standard (Corsairs only)   **25 points**
The legendary standard of Kaldour the Visionary, this banner carries the device of a monstrous serpent.

The unit is subject to the rules for Frenzy.

Banner of Murder   **25 points**
This standard is steeped in the blood of sacrificial victims, its murderous aura instilling a thirst for death and carnage in those carrying it aloft.

A unit with the Banner of Murder gains the Armour Piercing rule.

Banner of Cold Blood (One use only)   **15 points**
Soaked in the blood of slaughtered Lizardmen, the presence of the Banner of Cold Blood imbues those who carry it with cold-blooded discipline.

Announce that the unit is using the banner at the start of any player turn. For the duration of that turn, the unit containing the banner takes any Leadership tests on 3D6 and the Dark Elves player discards the highest D6 roll before comparing the score to the unit's Leadership value.

REFERENCE

CHARACTERS	M	WS	BS	S	T	W	I	A	Ld	Page
Crone Hellebron	5	7	6	4	3	3	9	4	10	66
Death Hag	5	6	6	4	3	2	8	3	9	50
Cauldron of Blood (Hag)	5	4	4	3	3	1	6	2	8	51
Lokhir Fellheart	5	6	6	4	3	2	7	3	9	69
Malekith	5	8	6	5	4	3	8	4	10	64
Malus Darkblade	5	6	5	4	3	2	7	3	9	67
Spite	7	3	0	4	4	1	2	2	4	67
Master	5	6	6	4	3	2	7	3	9	60
Morathi	5	5	4	3	3	3	6	3	10	65
Sulephet	8	4	0	4	4	3	4	3	6	65
Dreadlord	5	7	6	4	3	3	8	4	10	60
Shadowblade	6	10	10	4	3	2	10	3	10	68
Sorceress	5	4	4	3	3	2	5	1	8	62
Supreme Sorceress	5	4	4	3	3	3	5	1	9	62

CORE UNITS	M	WS	BS	S	T	W	I	A	Ld	Page
Assassin	5	9	9	4	3	2	10	3	10	61
Black Ark Corsairs	5	4	4	3	3	1	5	1	8	45
Reaver	5	4	4	3	3	1	5	2	8	45
Dark Rider	5	4	4	3	3	1	5	1	8	49
Herald	5	4	5	3	3	1	5	2	8	49
Dark Steed	9	3	0	3	3	1	4	1	5	56
Harpy	5	3	0	3	3	1	5	2	6	55
Crossbowman	5	4	4	3	3	1	5	1	8	44
Guardmaster	5	4	5	3	3	1	5	1	8	44
Warrior	5	4	4	3	3	1	5	1	8	44
Lordling	5	4	4	3	3	1	5	2	8	44

MOUNTS	M	WS	BS	S	T	W	I	A	Ld	Page
Black Dragon	6	6	0	6	6	6	3	5	8	57
Cold One	7	3	0	4	4	1	2	1	3	55

	M	WS	BS	S	T	W	I	A	Ld	Page
Manticore	6	5	0	5	5	4	5	4	5	59
Dark Pegasus	8	3	0	4	4	3	4	2	6	56
Dark Steed	9	3	0	3	3	1	4	1	5	56

SPECIAL UNITS	M	WS	BS	S	T	W	I	A	Ld	Page
Black Guard of Naggarond	5	5	4	3	3	1	6	2	9	46
Tower Master	5	5	4	3	3	1	6	3	9	46
Kouran of the Black Guard	5	5	4	3	3	1	6	3	9	70
Cold One Chariot	-	-	-	5	5	4	-	-	-	53
Charioteer	-	5	4	4	-	-	6	1	9	53
Cold One	7	3	0	4	-	-	2	1	-	55
Cold One Knights	5	5	4	4	3	1	6	1	9	52
Dread Knight	5	5	4	4	3	1	6	2	9	52
Cold One	7	3	0	4	4	1	2	1	3	55
Har Ganeth Executioners	5	5	4	4	3	1	5	1	8	47
Draich-master	5	5	4	4	3	1	5	2	8	47
Tullaris of Har Ganeth	5	5	4	4	3	1	5	2	8	71
Shade	5	5	5	3	3	1	5	1	8	48
Bloodshade	5	5	6	3	3	1	5	2	8	48
Witch Elf	5	4	4	3	3	1	6	1	8	50
Hag	5	4	4	3	3	1	6	2	8	50

RARE	M	WS	BS	S	T	W	I	A	Ld	Page
Reaper Bolt Thrower	-	-	-	-	7	3	-	-	-	54
Dark Elf	5	4	4	3	3	1	5	1	8	54
Karond Kar War Hydra	6	4	0	5	5	5	2	7	6	58
Beastmaster	6	4	4	3	3	1	5	2	8	58

By: Gav Thorpe.

Original Book by: Jervis Johnson. **Additional Material:** Robin Cruddace. **Cover Art:** Paul Dainton. **Illustration:** John Blanche, Alex Boyd, Paul Dainton, Dave Gallagher, Nuala Kinrade & Robin Carey. **Graphic Design:** Neil Hodgson & Tim Vincent. **Hobby Material:** Dave Andrews, Mark Jones & Chad Mierzwa. **Miniatures Sculptors:** Alexander Hedström, Ally Morrison, Brian Nelson, Juan Diaz, Mark Harrison, Martin Footitt, Michael Anderson, Jes Goodwin & Trish Morrison. **'Eavy Metal:** Neil Green, Keith Robertson, Kirsten Williams, Darren Latham, Fil Dunn, Anja Wettergren & Joe Tomaszewski. **Production Lead:** Tim Vincent. **Photography:** Stuart White & Ian Strickland. **Production:** Simon Burton, Chris Eggar & Emma Parrington. **Sub-editor:** Andrew Kenrick. **Thanks to our playtesters:** Adi McWalter, Brian Folcarelli, Conrad Gonsalves, Guy Grandison, Mark Havener, Kevin Coleman, Marko Lukic, Pete Scholey & Roy Eggensperger. **Special Thanks To:** Jeremy Vetock, Graham Davey, Alan Merrett, Rick Priestley, John Blanche, Martin Morrin & Mark Farr.

UK	US	Canada	Australia	Northern Europe
Games Workshop Ltd., Willow Rd, Lenton, Nottingham. NG7 2WS	Games Workshop Inc., 6711 Baymeadow Drive, Glen Burnie, Maryland 21060-6401	Games Workshop, 2679 Bristol Circle, Unit 3, Oakville, Ontario, L6H 6Z8	Games Workshop, 23 Liverpool Street, Ingleburn, NSW 2565	Games Workshop Ltd., Willow Rd, Lenton, Nottingham. NG7 2WS, UK

Produced by Games Workshop